THE
SILLY MIND

—⊃◦◦◦⊂—

LEARNING
TO TAKE LIFE
More or *Less*
SERIOUSLY

THE
SILLY MIND

LEARNING
TO TAKE LIFE
More or Less
SERIOUSLY

David R. Lima, M.S.W.
and
Donald N. Scobel, M.S.S.A.

Super Six Publishing

THE SILLY MIND: Learning to Take Life More or Less Seriously
First Printing 1997, Revised Edition 2000
Copyright 1997, 1999 by David R. Lima and Donald N. Scobel
Printed in the United States of America

ISBN 1-893733-01-7 Paperback

SUPER SIX PUBLISHING
8353 MENTOR AVE.
MENTOR, OHIO 44060
A Division of David R. Lima, ACSW, Inc.
www.lima-associates.com
(800) 810-9011

*Although The Silly Mind provides accurate and authoritative infor-
mation concerning the topics covered, it does not take the place of a
competent professional in the event counseling or other professional
services are required. This book does not constitute, and should not
be construed as, the practice of any regulated profession.*

ACKNOWLEDGMENTS

The authors gratefully acknowledge those individuals instrumental in the development of twentieth century psychotherapy. Among those with whom we have had special working relationships and have gleaned much from our association are Albert Ellis, Michael Mahoney, Jay Haley, Arnold Lazarus, James Bard, Raymond DiGiuseppe, Robert Neimeyer, Joan Borysenko, Janet Wolfe, David Burns, Francine Shapiro, Claudia Black, Richard Gardner, Donald Meichenbaum, Peggy Papp, Bill O'Hanlon, Cloe Madanes, Neil Jacobson, Michael Hoyt, Michele Weiner-Davis, Kenneth Sewell and Joseph LoPicolo. Each interaction provided more grist for our mill and encouraged us in our efforts to write this book.

Cover Art By Gary Causer

a•bsurd adj. [< Fr.>] "The state or condition in which a person exists in an irrational and meaningless universe and the person's life has no meaning outside of his or her existence."
-ab•surd´i•ty

A NOTE ABOUT PRONOUNS

This book is written in the first and second person...mainly to personalize it, but also to avoid the gender-specific third person. We have not attempted to identify which author is associated with a particular experience. We use the first person pronoun "I" rather indescriminantly. We think it would be "silly" otherwise.

TABLE OF CONTENTS

CHAPTER 4
LOST AND FOUND: HIDING OUR PAINFUL ABSURDITIES   53

I can't remember where I put my socks, so how can I remember where I put several thousands of absurdities?

CHAPTER 5
THE ART OF DEFUSING A PAINFUL ABSURDITY   63

Do people ever really change their mind? Ha!

CHAPTER 6
PUTTING AN ABSURDITY ON THE WITNESS STAND   75

Perry Mason-izing a belief, putting its feet to the fire.

ABOUT THE AUTHORS, ABOUT THE BOOK

DON SCOBEL

Dave Lima and I have agreed to express what in our lives has brought us to this point of writing a book together...particularly a book that interweaves philosophy, mental health and a fresh therapeutic approach. I suspect my road has more twists. I am more wizened, if not wisdom-ed than my co-author.

I began my professional career as a chemist, at least academically. I received a Bachelor's degree in that subject, behaving quite well at bookwork, but like a wild bull in the laboratory. I own the college record for glass breakage. I couldn't quite measure out the right amount of things. Mine was the only laboratory-made coffee that no fellow student would imbibe. My college did bestow a degree upon me, but with the unqualifiable agreement, signed with my own glass-cut blood, that I would never in my life again step foot in a laboratory.

From there I spent a quarter century in the field of labor relations in its pinnacle days which coal miner advocate, John L. Lewis, described as "labor and its adversaries locked in deadly embrace." I learned from many negotiating experiences that fairness is illusive, and varies widely from where you sit at the table. It was in these worklife wars where the notion of absurdity became clear to me...that we are quick to see the absurdity of another's view, but blind to the absurdity of our own. Conflict resolution was the arena in which I first gleaned the uniqueness of the meaning we each give to events. No universal resolutions floating out there in space!

I proceeded then to manage my own consulting firm in the area of people relationships...dedicated to the idea that class

differences and favoritisms in the workplace are counterpro-
ductive. The more the decision-making is dispersed to those
who do the work, and the rewards shared accordingly, the more
the enterprise will flourish. I even wrote a book from my zeal
for this perspective (Creative Worklife). Here, again, I found
an absence of widespread acceptance. This egalitarian ethic
was situationally received or rejected. No magic ether. No
universal truth!

During much of this time I pursued a theater avocation.
Later in life I ran a dinner theater where I produced, directed
and often took a role. Acting was my first love...climbing into
the persona of another being, thinking his thoughts, feeling his
feelings, doing the things he was created to do...an absorption
in another's skin. Directing captured me as well...digging into
each character; understanding their interconnectedness. A good
playwright discerns that given a common experience, each of
the players create their own significance of that experience.
Theater is absurd. That "All the world's a stage" is the grandest absurdity of them all.

Then I switched my trade once more; a student again after
four decades...two grueling years to become a mental health
therapist. I am not long in the tooth in direct practice, but my
other career and life experiences are in the room with me. At
first I found myself borrowing broadly from all the great psychotherapies; cognitive, gestalt, behavioral, rational-emotive,
object relations, solution focused, client centered...all absurd
actually, if you reject the arrogance of a universal truth. *The
Silly Mind* intends to draw from many concepts to provide a
simple way for people to understand the meaning they have put
on their lives. If that meaning is not serving them well, they
can alter it to better serve their life journey. Thus here I am -
pen in hand.

DAVE LIMA

My journey began in 1964 as a graduate social work student at Florida State University. I was the first in the history of my family to go to college, by the way, which was as much the dream of my progenitors as my own. Armed with a Master's degree, I began my clinical work in the mental health system in my home state of Ohio.

In the late '60s and in the '70s, I was mostly involved in public service and helped start up a Free Clinic in Lake County, Ohio. In 1979, I went "private" - mostly because, family in hand, money became a point of interest in a classically under-rewarded profession. I chose solo private practice with a determination to help people get better and reduce their emotional disturbances quickly. Born out of necessity and my own philosophical bent, brief therapy was the key to a successful private practice. This is becoming even more emphasized in today's arena of care. I enrolled in the Associate Fellowship Training Program at the Institute for Rational-Emotive (and now -Behavioral) Therapy in New York and completed this post-graduate training in 1986.

Afterwards, I attempted my first continuing professional education workshop. This educational aspect of my practice has now expanded to include over twenty nationally recognized behavioral healthcare leaders who conduct continuing education workshops throughout the United States. I have learned a great deal from my relationships with these leaders, but most importantly from Albert Ellis.

So here Don and I are, writing a book, *The Silly Mind*. For me, absurdity therapy is a natural outgrowth of the cognitive approach to life adjustment problems. In a nutshell, our thinking gets stuck in a place that generates unpleasant feelings and unproductive behaviors. I have been working with absurdity therapy clinically for years without defining it as systematically as we do in this book. What has become clear to me is that I have yet to find a single value a person gives to his or her life experiences that is accepted universally. If this is the case, then all of our beliefs are absurd - not having a pervasive meaning outside of our own minds. This concept of absurdity has helped many people in my practice take themselves less inflexibly, recognizing they can change their own beliefs, their own absurdities in a way that uplifts their moods and their behaviors. How this is done - and how you can do it yourself - is the essence of this book

FOREWORD

This is an unusually good, brief, pithy, and useful book. It clearly and absorbingly presents one of the main ideas that is explicitly and/or implicitly made in virtually all effective psychotherapies: the idea that, most fortunately, people largely create their own emotional and behavioral disturbances; and that, therefore, they can, even more fortunately, effectively reduce these difficulties and make themselves less disturbed. Does this mean you? Yes! David Lima and Donald Scobel not only lucidly make this point, but show you what to do about it and how to undisturb yourself about the frequent problems you will doubtless encounter during your lifetime.

Will this important view of human upsetness seem familiar to those of you who know my own writings and cassettes on rational emotive behavior therapy (REBT)? Indeed it will, as I have promulgated it for over forty years in many REBT articles and books. But don't forget that I largely derived it from the writings of many ancient and modern philosophers—some of whom are also quoted in *The Silly Mind*. Another commonality between my views and those of the authors of this book: we arrived at the wisdom described herein through learning by our own experiences and considering the emotional problems of our friends and clients. We saw from these experiences that we and others are prone to construct many absurd views of ourselves, of other people, and of external conditions and that these absurdities, and not merely the unfortunate events that occur in our lives, unduly upset us. And we concluded that we can thereby change ourselves and our self-sabotaging reactions.

This is the important lesson that Lima and Scobel keep emphasizing in their well-written book. No, Ms. Anxiety and Mr. Depression, you don't just get upset by your parents, teachers, friends, and coworkers who, to be sure, often plague you. Instead, you mainly consciously and unconsciously, and quite absurdly, choose to upset yourself. Good! Because you can also, as a born constructivist and problem solver, choose to reduce your emotional problems, make yourself—as I keep insisting in REBT—much less disturbable, and propel yourself on your way to a more fulfilling and self-actualizing existence.

Yes, you can, provided of course, that you follow the three major insights of rational emotive behavior therapy, which the authors keep stressing in this book: 1) You usually are self-upsettable as a result of creating your own absurdities; 2) Even though you may have learned and created self-defeating ideas in your childhood and adolescence, you still unthinkingly and rigidly tend to hold many of them today; and 3) Clearly seeing this, as *The Silly Mind* consistently shows you how to do, requires you to use the wisdom in this book. Continuing to work and practice at doing so will more effectively help you do the trick.

So read about your absurdities in Lima and Scobel's fine book. Observe that you still, right now, idiotically believe them. Work and practice at firmly challenging, questioning, disputing, and disbelieving them until you get and keep yourself on the road to much fewer emotional doldrums. This is what *The Silly Mind* shows you how to do. Read it and think!

Albert Ellis, Ph.D., President
Albert Ellis Institute for Rational
Emotive Behavior Therapy
45 East 65th Street
New York, NY 10021

THE
SILLY MIND

LEARNING TO TAKE LIFE
More or Less
SERIOUSLY

INTRODUCTION

THE SILLY MIND

The working title of this book was "Absurdity Therapy," a very practical title since that was what we were talking about: how we can each get ourselves out of troubling feelings and behaviors by examining the way we think, our beliefs, or what we are calling our ABSURDITIES. But when the work was done and it came time to give it an official title, "Absurdity Therapy" sounded dry to us, without the lightness or humor we hope the work embraces. So we looked for alternatives and with the help of wife and daughters came up with *The Silly Mind*, probably for no other reason than it's silly. So then we tacked on the sub-title, *Learning to Take Life More or Less Seriously*...which more precisely reflects our tale.

WHOSE BELIEF IS ABSURD?

Remember the childhood verse:
"Spring is here. Spring is here.
The bird is on the wing.
How absurd. How absurd.
The wing is on the bird."

Setting aside for the moment the expression "on the wing" in the sense of taking flight, we are presented here with an issue of interpreting the juxtaposition of the wing and the rest of the bird.

One person might say the wing is clearly on the bird. After all, the body is the true bulk of the bird and its wings are appendages. Thinking otherwise is absurd. No! says another - the essence of "bird" is its capacity for flight, thus its wings are its essence. The rest of the bird is subservient to its wings and to think otherwise is absurd. Which view is foolish, nonsensical?   From each point of view, the other is absurd. Could they both be caricatures?

We think so. The oppositional viewers in this case might draw or photograph the exact same bird...they might even agree that the structure of that bird is universally accepted...or close to it. What differs is the meaning, the significance, the interpretation of "bird" - and that is a personal matter. Since there is obviously no universal MEANING of that bird, then each person's personalized version will be considered with some measure of absurdity by those who give it a different meaning.

THE MEANINGLESSNESS OF CRUEL DISEASES

We see so much of this in therapy, working with terminally ill cancer patients for example. Two people, close in age, have the same malady...of the same organ...with the same medically predicted shortening of life. The science of their situation is alike, or similar. One says, "So my life is shortened. We all die one time or another. I'm privileged to know when my time is up. I have some things I want to do; some people I want to hug; some others to tell I'm sorry; some affairs to straighten up; some to let know my dying is okay with me."

Another says, "O my God I'm going to die. I'll suffer. Others will see me suffer. The pain will be terrible. I'll waste away like a living corpse. My loved ones will be agonized. It's awful. God give me the strength to take my own life quickly."

The cancer, the imminency of death, is alike for these two, but the meaning is vastly divergent. Whose meaning is absurd? In the absence of a universal meaning, are not both meanings absurd from the viewpoint of the other? Are not each the author of the significance they give to their own cancer, their own absurdity?...and if they are the author, might they not be able to change the script if their absurdity is not serving them well - is causing them grief and misery?

ISSUES

These are the kinds of issues that *The Silly Mind* addresses. It is a process for uncovering or identifying our own absurdities; for recognizing that the interpretation, the significance we give to events and experiences is not bound or predestined by a universal proclamation. We can take the measure of our own meanings and decide whether they are helping us get to where we want to go - or stopping us in our tracks - or promoting our discontent. Knowing this, there is a process for altering our absurdities, however minutely, to have us feel the way we want to feel; to get where we want to go; to enrich relationships; to protect ourselves from harm; to minimize the discomfort and enhance the joy of the journey.

ABSURDITY FROM THE THRESHOLD OF SPACE

One other anecdote may help put *The Silly Mind* in perspective. I had the occasion a few years ago to fly from

London to New York (in less than three hours) on the super-sonic Concorde. The early part of the flight was unremark-able. The take-off and ascent were not much different from an ordinary jet flight. There was a mock-speed counter vis-ible on the front panel of the plane. I braced myself for some vibration when we pierced the sound barrier. There was none. I looked out the small window. We were over what seemed to be a high level of clouds. There was no sensation of ex-cessive speed.

I settled down to be served an elegant cuisine, an ex-quisite Bordeaux, when I took another look out of the oval window. The clouds had disappeared and to my absolute amazement I was sure I could see the curvature of the earth. It was startling, like seeing a small crescent of the moon...except the crescent was a blue-white swirl we have come to see in many astronaut's photographs. This crescent - earth - was enveloped in the darkness of space. I went hollow in the pit of my stomach like feeling the first descent in the first car of a giant roller-coaster. The feeling passed but the wonder of the moment lingered. I was on the brink of the fourth dimension, the space through which the earth hurls in its endless pursuit of time.

There was no feeling of supremeness...quite different.

There was a pervasive emptiness, the earth a whirling crescent. If anything was on it, it was insignificant. No wars. No governments. No politics. No disease. No reli-gion. Sphere and space, but no meaning. Is this not an el-egant absurdity...trying to ascribe an ultimate meaning to a meaningless universe...like thinking what any one person be-lieves is an ultimate truth. How absurd.

The Silly Mind works on different levels. At the per-sonal level it operates on the notion we are free to interpret the sense of whatever happens to us, so we might as well interpret it to our humor, to our happiness. At the grand or spacial level we are given structure, light and darkness, mat-ter and science...yet most of all...the freedom to tell our own speck of a story....no need to bow down to a vast intention.

A PROCESS PRIMER

As *The Silly Mind* unfolds it will be seen not as theory, but as a primer. We have applied absurdity therapy with people who declare themselves bogged down by depression, anxiety, panic, anger, traumatic stress, obsessions, relation-ship failures, fears, losses. People can mend themselves - alter their meanings - apply their own absurdity therapy. We have some "how to" ideas, developed with the many people who have let us help them. It is not a step by step prescrip-tion. That would be absurd. YES, WE CONFESS *THE SILLY MIND* IS ITSELF AN ABSURDITY. We must each give it its own meaning. We only ask for you to walk with us a little while - knowing surely you are ever walking your own way.

CHAPTER 1

WHAT DO YOU MEAN MY THINKING IS ABSURD?
THERE ARE NO UNIVERSAL MEANINGS

The absurd is the essential concept and the first truth.
- Albert Camus (1942)

DEFINITIONS

According to most dictionaries, the word "absurd" has two meanings. The first is the more common usage: "ridiculously unreasonable"...usually followed with a number of synonyms like foolish, incongruous, inconsistent, senseless, wild, nonsensical. Most of us are quite familiar with this definition. For example, somebody says something that rings unlikely to us: "New York City is getting cleaner every day," To this we say, or think to ourselves, "That's absurd."

The other definition of absurd is a leap into the core of our very existence. Webster's New Collegiate Dictionary defines "absurd" secondly as: "The state or condition in which a person exists in an irrational and meaningless universe and the person's life has no meaning outside of his or her existence."

Now, that is a leap indeed! From a launch pad of the ridiculous, our very "aliveness" is hurled far beyond the sublime into a vast and universal meaninglessness called...the absurd. Even our existence is absurd!

There is no necessary linkage between the multiple definitions of a single word. More often than not, the separate definitions do not relate to one another. There is no junction, for example, between the cast of a play and a cast into which molten metal is poured.

The two definitions of absurd, however, seem to have an elegance in their juxtaposition, perhaps too elegant to ignore: like a telescope with foolishness at the small end and a vast meaninglessness at the large end.

In similar fashion there is a duality in each of us. We are who we are inside our body, under our skin, so to speak. This is the small end of the telescope, the foolish end; not literally, of course, but poetically, like Shakespeare's "...we are come to this great stage of fools." No one else is at this small end of the telescope, only the entity I call "me."

Yet we don't quite exist inside our body alone. We also exist - or mingle - in an environment outside of our body in what we are calling the universe. This universe is literally all the things beyond our skin, from a distant star to an object, say this book, close to us at the moment. This is the big end of the telescope. This is the definition of absurd relating to a universe that has no meaning, no proclamations, no neon signs telling us what to do, what to think, what it's all about. This is the grand absurdity of our existence.

NO UNIVERSAL MEANING?

True, the things outside of us have no universal meaning, absolutely none, say we absurdists. By "meaning" in this usage we are not talking about the definition of something, like a door means a barrier by which entry is opened or closed. We are talking evaluatively, the idea something conveys to the mind. For example, a door enables me to get on with my life, to move in and out of experiences. Another might say a door lets me walk away from my troubles. We once had a client who said, "I'm done counseling...I'm giving you the door!" When we say there is no universal meaning, we are saying there is no pervasive all embracing significance to any of the events or experiences that we have in our entire lifetime. The significance we give to things is

OUR significance. Okay, a few others may ascribe the same or similar significance to that event - but not everyone, thank goodness.

In a sense, this gives us each an awesome power. Even though astronomers speculate there are as many galaxies in the universe as there are billions of stars in our own galaxy, each of us - specks actually - have the capacity to give this incredible expanse and everything in it whatever significance we choose. The "what it's all about?" comes strictly from inside our skin.

Most of us do in fact exercise our option to give the universe a meaning. We may call it our religion or philosophy or just our big picture. This license, however, has an implied application that touches us closer to home than interpreting the celestial universe. If we alone can give a meaning to the universe, then we alone can give a meaning to our own particular lives. We alone assign meaning, a personal significance, to an old pair of shoes in the attic, the bed we sleep in, the big tree in the back yard, our relationship with aunt Martha, the gravy boat passed down to us by our great grandmother, the election of 1996. Like the universe, everything we do or that's done to us, has no meaning "out there." When it comes to the significance of things, each human being is the center of the universe. We are at the same time a tiny pebble...and the universal interpreter. Now that - by definition - is absurd.

YOU AND I SEE THE SAME PICTURE ON THE WALL

A ready distinction is made here between the substance and the meaning of things. Astronomers constantly uncover added information about the substance and structure of the universe and we accept their revised model, quite universally, until further revisions come along. Generally speaking, we agree more about the descriptive world than the evaluative world. This is not to underrate descriptive differences, however. That our descriptions of things are incomplete and seen differently by different observers is what spawns our never ending research. When I look up at the heavens at night, it sure looks like the stars are revolving around us. Thank goodness fellows like Capurnicus and Galileo saw it differently. Another example is that our court system mainly exists to resolve differences in the description of the same event by different people.

Given these descriptive differences, however, the significance or meaning we give to the same or similar events are far more diverse and individualized than our description of those events. No universal meaning. Thus, by definition, all the personal meanings we give to things - are ABSURD.

If you and I look at the same picture on a wall, we will see the same picture - more or less, even given our differences in eyesight. We won't argue that it's a man, mid-thirties, blond wavy hair, mustache, wire-rim glasses, pointed chin, shirt and tie. It is the significance of that picture, what it means to us personally, the priority we assign to it, that defies commonality and yet - in the final analysis - guides our lives.

One person might say "That picture of a man on the wall...my father...died when I was a boy. Greatest man on earth. His memory will guide me always."

Another person looking at the same picture says "Humph! My business partner. Greediest man alive. Watched him every minute or he'd rob me blind!"

Whose meaning is absurd? They both are - in a universe of no immortal meanings.

ARE ALL THE MEANINGS WE GIVE TO THINGS... ASURDITIES?

As defined here, yes...not reflecting a universal significance. When it comes to playing a baseball game, you and I might be on the same team, cheering each other on. But when it comes time to assign a significance to that game, (or any experience), we each climb back into our own skin.

BUT WHY ABSURD?

If the significance we each give to things is intra-personal, why don't we just characterize this meaning as non-universal or non-reflective or unique? Why absurd?

Since we have defined absurdity therapy as a process for freshening up our lives, it will encourage us to examine some of the meanings we have given things, especially those that have un-freshened our lives, ladened us down. From our experience as therapists, people are not as inclined to bond themselves as tightly to what they consider absurdities in their lives...as they do to their life meanings. Absurdities are often silly, laughable, discardable. Meanings are ponderous, imbedded, holy, immutable. Seeing our meanings as absurdities - and they are - makes us more amenable to reexamine them, bend them, toss them out if need be. Also, we are more readily inclined to see absurdity in the beliefs of others than in ourselves. If we consider meanings as absurdities in general - across the board - as applicable to ourself as anyone, we are better prepared for our own scrutiny.

There is an inner-humor in the notion of absurdity. Comedians make a living from their keen eye for the absurd. Jack Benny tells the story of walking down a street in one of the movie studio compounds dressed for his movie part; wearing a three cornered fool's hat with bells at the tips, clown-like pantaloons and a shirt flowing widely in the arms and shoulders. His friend George Burns passed him walking in the other direction. With just a fleeting glance, George said, "you working?" and continued on his way. Benny said he walked two blocks before he realized Burns had zapped him again: "Telling me I AM a fool, not just dressed as one...Well!" It seems to us life isn't much fun unless we see some fun in it. Some experiences are unpleasant, even tragic, and however absurd they may be, it is not easy to grace them with any humor. But the more we are able to see our beliefs, our meanings, as absurd, it can often take the edge off their somberness. We have noticed in those of our friends who take their lives most gracefully in stride, they sense the inner humor of their own absurdities. They have had some tough experiences and losses in their lives that have had them feel awful. But they also have a way of tweaking these particular absurdities...giving them a small turn sometimes, or chucking them entirely, that has let them move forward again. It is the absurdity awareness of people who get on well in life that has encouraged us to study the absurdity phenomena. There are ways to identify and unclog those absurdities that have you stuck in a negative mode.

ARE ABSURDITIES CHANGEABLE?

We think most people alter and discard absurdities every day, sometimes every hour. We reflect on the years a friend harbored a hateful meaning of snow for the myriad of discomforts it fostered upon him. Then, later in life, he discovered skiing...the discomforts have faded from his meaning, replaced by the vision of an absolutely perfect downhill run...moguls be warned! Snow now lifts his spirits to the mountain top.

In this case a new event helped change an old meaning. Often no new event is needed. Reflection is sufficient. How many times have you gone to a movie...and come out saying it was awful. Later you discover some aspect of that movie is staying with you, moving you, giving you some exciting new insight...and you say to someone "you've got to see this great movie!" Sometimes our first impression of a person is lasting. Sometimes it isn't. We may revise the meaning that person has in our lives several times. Since we write the meaning of events in our lives, we are free to change the script, sometimes with the flick of the mind. Admittedly, this is not always so easy. We have seen in many people with life adjustment problems, some severely dysfunctional, the inability to discern an absurdity locked inside them, or if they do discern it , they can't alter it. They chiseled it in hard stone within them. Yet the chisel remains in their own hands. Absent some physiological barriers, there are few immutable absurdities. We may not be able to change the events in our lives, but we are the master of their meaning...their absurdity.

A CONTRARY VIEW OF THE ABSURD

There are some who believe the basic questions of our existence are the driving force of our anxieties, and to protect ourselves from being overwhelmed by these anxieties, we create a host of defenses that may or may not serve us well. Among the existential issues are a natural fear of death; a deep sense of isolation from existing only inside our own skin; the awesome responsibility of being free to assign our own meanings to a meaningless universe. We would not deny that these can be frightening, awesome issues, but that they are universal drivers of anxiety seems itself in contradiction with an absence of universal meaning. We have known and worked with people (including ourselves) who give divergent personal significance to these issues, including death, and have altered their significance on one or more occasions in their lives.

We think the idea of existential drivers of anxiety is absurd. But then, we gladly accept that our own ideas are absurd. Thus our chorus once again: No Universal Meaning! If absurdity therapy helps you manage the significance of events to enhance your joy in life, then we are a good read...however absurd.

IN A NUTSHELL

Absurdity therapy is recognizing that the significance we put on things makes no sense in a grand way outside of our own skin. There are no "one size fits all" meanings. Since we are the creator and keeper of the significance we give to objects and events, we can also evaluate if those meanings are helping us live a pleasant, fruitful life...or holding us back in some kind of despair. If some of the meanings we give to things are serving us poorly, we have the power to alter or discard them. We need not drown in the stream of our discontent. The absurd is our foolishness at one end and the significance we give the universe at the other end. *The Silly Mind* is a way to manage what Albert Camus calls absurdity: the "essential concept", the "first truth" within ourselves.

CHAPTER 2

———◁◦◦◦▷———

THE LINK-PIN BETWEEN FEELINGS AND ABSURDITIES
OUR FEELINGS EMERGE FROM WHAT WE BELIEVE ABOUT THE EVENTS OF LIFE

The brain is in the body, but not the mind. The body is in the mind.

- Unknown

FEELINGS: TO WHOM DO THEY BELONG?

As I am author of my absurdities - the significance I give to events in my life - I am also the author of what I am feeling at any moment in my life. If I am sad, I am the one feeling the sadness. If I am angry, I might want to blame that anger on what someone else has said or done, but I own that feeling of anger; it is in my person, mine alone, and no one else can feel that anger for me. Similarly someone might want to cheer me up, do all kinds of nutty things to uplift me...but, indeed, if my spirits rise and I feel a joy within me, it is my joy and I alone can feel that feeling for myself.

Forest Gump may have moved me to tears, but the tears were MINE. I am the possessor of my passions. Absurd? Yes. But an absurdity most of us can't refute.

We may attribute the source of a feeling to something that happens outside of ourselves, but we're the ones who pull that feeling out of our internal file drawer and insert it in the active slot. It is sometimes difficult to separate the event from the feeling. The death of my uncle depresses me terribly. The driver who cut in front of me enrages me. The person in the alley frightens me out of my wits.

True, there may be a linkage between my depression and my uncle's death, my rage and the conduct of the other driver, my fright and the person in the alley...but in each case I am the one who cranks up the feeling and feeds it to my nervous system. Other people in similar situations might crank up different feelings. Their feelings are their feelings and mine are mine. Again, there are no universal feelings attached to any event. The significance of the event and any feeling related to the event are of my own authorship, my own absurdity and my own personal emotion.

THE RELATIONSHIP BETWEEN ABSURDITIES AND FEELINGS

We have had experiences where a feeling seemed to pop into us, like awakening from a deep sleep feeling sad...or contemplative. Even if we try to hook that feeling to some event or thought, nothing seems to match up, the feeling was...just there. We can be content not caring where it came from.

This doesn't happen often, however, and if we work at it, we can usually link that feeling back to one of our absurdities. Chances are...it is the significance we have put on some event in our life that has us feeling the way we do. Our absurdities are like file-keepers of the drawers of our emotions. They are the ones who open up the drawer and pull out "happiness" or "perplexed" or "jealousy" or "fear" or "ecstasy." The loss of a football game because the referees made a bunch of lousy calls - pulls up anger, resentment, maybe even vengeance. The loss of a football game because the best team won - pulls up disappointment, respect and a zest to improve. It isn't the loss, but what that loss means to us that determines the feeling.

A common misconception is that the event, the thing that happened to us - or is happening - or may happen - or will happen - or we imagine could happen - is what generates our feelings. The storm frightens me. The sexual contemplation excites me. The sunset calms me. The football loss angers me.

The fallacy of this notion comes back to our initial premise: No Universal Meaning! No single event means the same thing to everyone, nor does it generate a universal feeling. Thus the event may be involved, but standing alone, it does not turn on our feeling switch.

I remember being in a park where people had congregated to watch Fourth of July fireworks. Each colorful blast was accompanied by a chorus of "oohs" and "aahs." Most of the people in that park felt a similar sense of wonder and elation at those colorful, explosive patterns. But not all. When I looked about, I watched an older man slowly slump in his folding chair and fall asleep - snoring. A young nearby couple was passionately kissing, either oblivious to the fireworks or imagining them as their private orchestra! Two children, arm-wrestling, were still locked in their arduous battle. A woman was shouting at the man at her side to go get hamburgers before the fireworks were over and "everyone rushes to McDonald's." Obviously the fireworks were not generating the same feeling in everyone.

Recalling the previously mentioned picture of a man on the wall, the person who sees his beloved, departed father probably feels a bittersweetness, a longing and endearing. The person who sees his cheating business partner probably feels a tinge of satisfaction; "I wouldn't wish anyone dead, but if it happens to someone it should be a crook like him!"

Also, for each of these viewers the feeling might be quite different when looking at the same picture a few weeks later, or a year later - again indicating it is not just the act of looking at the picture that conjures up the feeling.

Clearly, it is not the event that has kindled the feeling, but the significance we have put on the event. Our absurdity, if you will, taps into our emotional pool. What a blessing when you think about it. If the event itself caused the feeling, we would be stuck with that pain forever. We can't

change what happened to us, but we can alter the significance we put on it. In order to moderate the feeling, we can
tweak our absurdities good and proper - and why not!
They're absurd anyway!

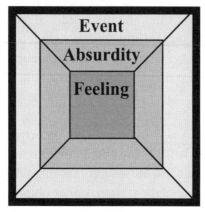

Figure 1

Admittedly, this chain of events, or rather this chain from
events to feelings, is central also to cognitive and rational
emotive behavioral therapy. *The Silly Mind* simply adds that
an absurdity is just that, an absurdity; our "significance of
an event" is absurd, nothing vast or eternal, nothing ponderous or immutable - but rather at our whim. We whip up our
absurdities in the kitchen of our mind. We can take out some
of this, add a pinch of that, freeze it , braise it, even throw it
out if its taste is too bitter or its swallow no longer digest-
ible. This is the incredible power we have to make ourselves
content - even in unpleasant circumstances.

WHAT IS THE RECIPE FOR AFFIRMATIVE AB-SURDITIES?

We made reference earlier to absurdities that move us
forward and those that hold us back, those that bring out our
inner-humorist and those that bore us and bog us down. What
makes the distinction? What are the ingredients of absurdities that help us get to where we want to go?

The response varies by individual, of course. That which moves us closer to what's important to us in our life journey is an affirming absurdity. Conversely, that which keeps us away from what's important to us in life is a negative absurdity; it delays or denies our desired end.

We believe there are four fundamental characteristics of a belief that help move people to where they want to go. These characteristics, or values, constitute the value system of absurdity therapy, generally.

These values are certainly not universal and thus are, themselves, absurd. They are, however, our guiding lights. If your "value absurdities" diverge substantially from these, in a different ballpark, so to speak, then *The Silly Mind* is not for you. We suspect not too many of you will set us aside at this point.

We believe an absurdity - to be affirming - needs to fulfill ALL of these characteristics:

Life Affirming: It is self-preserving, helps keep us alive or supports the absurdity we call life. It protects us from harm. Absurdity therapy is essentially for those who want to enrich their aliveness, who want to examine and if necessary alter their absurdities in a way to enhance not only the fact, but the quality of being alive. We realize there are some circumstances, like with the terminally ill cancer patients discussed earlier, where death acceptance rather than life affirmation is, per force, the affirming characteristic...and can be most affirming and calming indeed. However, affirming the life process is the substance of this value of *The Silly Mind*.

In Concert With Society: We know a few people who live reclusive lives and are quite content with their chosen circumstances. Yet, none of them are in total isolation, no matter how well they minimize their social interaction. Most of us, however, are in steady interaction with others. A characteristic of an affirming absurdity is that it doesn't dissuade this interactive process. We are talking of no deliberate harm to the human cause, a letting of life in others as in ourselves. We are talking of fair play: or - as much right for others to have their affirming absurdities as we are to have our own. This doesn't mean we must accept, or can't resist some societal norms, but that we won't take arms against them. This is the characteristic that takes murder and other anti-social behaviors off the list of life affirmations, even though some people may feel uplifted by extreme counter-social absurdities. This is an awareness that what uplifts the individual is not at the sacrifice of the social milieu. Absurdity therapy is committed to both individual and societal affirmation.

We are not suggesting here that a pervasive love of all humanity or an absence of competitiveness among people is required. We suspect most of us have some kind of heirarchy of people we care for. This is simply an affirmation of other peoples' rights in a common society.

Goal Achievement: That an affirmative absurdity moves a person toward the achievement of a life objective is its most obvious characteristic. It is also an illusive characteristic. Our aims in life are often in flux, altering as we have new experiences. We know of a person who wanted to be a dancer until he lost a leg in Viet Nam and then went on to become a choreographer!

The definition of a good goal is one that develops us for our next layer of goals. We are often in transition. However, it is still quite possible to detect whether the significance we have given an occurrence in our life - an absurdity - is moving us toward a place we want to go, or is holding us back, reining us in. We will talk more about goal establishing later (including short range goals, like smoking, that can have long range fatality), but suffice it for now to suggest that goal-striving gives us a life process and is, indeed, an important absurdity measure; an imperative for *The Silly Mind.*

Reducing Conflict: We would not suggest that all conflict is inappropriate. Some conflict is necessary to clearly delineate the absence of conflict, clear the pipes, so to speak. Some conflict illuminates issues for further discovery and helps people learn and grow. However, most life adjustment problems are punctuated by undesirable personal conflict, both inner conflict, self with self - and external conflict, self with something outside of our skin. Some of our absurdities are often enmeshed with these turbulent, upsetting conflicts. The significance we have given something in our life is holding us back, limiting our motion like an animal leashed to a tree. The extent to which we can uncover and alter these absurdities, or counterbalance them with new absurdities that minimize disturbing conflicts - is another absurdity measure and a critical value of *The Silly Mind*.

These four values - **life affirming, society affirming, goal achieving** and **conflict reducing** - characterize absurdities that carry us toward our life objectives. They are also the essential building blocks of absurdity therapy. No ponderous philosophy here. Quite simple really, unless you believe everything in your life is neatly laid out for you by a grand, universal plan!

This value context of absurdity therapy also speaks to those people, however few, who hold that an important element of their life journey is some kind of antisocial behavior - like racism, ostracism, a dictatorial sense of omnipotence, even murder. Can such notions be affirming absurdities for anyone? We think not, since they fall short of the value criterion of "society affirming," and usually these antisocial absurdities also fail the "conflict reducing" test.

This dilemma exists within all the helping professions. Does not medicine sometimes make a person healthier to do awful things? We do, after all, provide medical help to prisoners, even those who say when they get out they have a few more shops to rob. These are the kinds of ethical issues that urge any theory or scheme of things to have a value context, some basic tenets at their core. Again, not universal values, these are just the value absurdities embraced by *The Silly Mind*.

THE DENIAL—AFFIRMATION CONTINUUM

It would be nice to think our absurdities either affirm or oppose our life journey and throwing a switch can change the oppositional ones to affirmations. Of course, it's not that easy. We conceive that our absurdities lie on a continuum with firm affirmation at one end and deep denial on the other. We choose the word denial as the antonym of affirmation because "denial's" double meaning is most fitting. It means both "in opposition to" and, in the psychological sense, "disavowing or ignoring thoughts that evoke guilt or pain." In both these senses, they forestall our positive movement.

An absurdity might "deny" us access or progress toward our desired goal or affirmation. An absurdity might be so disaffirming that its very existence within us is "in denial", obscured within us like an invisible virus causing psychological pain...and sometimes the symptoms of physical sickness as well. This would be the Deep Denial end of the continuum. At the mid-point an absurdity is At Rest, moving us neither toward affirmation nor denial. This position can be very significant.

For example, a client of ours was "dropped" by his girlfriend who ran off with someone else. He gave that event a substantially denying significance, a negative absurdity; "I must be no good. I'm a worthless human being. No one will ever live with me again. It's what my mother did to my father." The client felt deeply depressed, even on the brink of hopelessness.

In a while however, he was able to bend that absurdity; "Well, she has walked out on other men so at least I'm not the only worthless human being. Another woman and I mutually broke off an earlier romance and both of us were able to get on and accept new people in our lives. My father got himself together when mom left." The client's feelings changed considerably. The hopelessness went away entirely. The depression eased to the point where he could sleep through the night and eat almost normally, and not feel that inner pain. What he had done was to neutralize that absurdity...bring it to the resting point. It wasn't affirming, he saw no advantage to the break-up, but it was no longer denying, dragging him down, interfering with his other activities. At Rest can be a much improved absurdity. It is often a position of calm.

In this particular case the man was able to alter the absurdity even further after a period of time. "No question the break-up was best for both of us. I wasn't ready to commit to her and her two young children. I learned a great deal about myself from her. I know it wouldn't have worked out in the long haul." He has nudged the original absurdity toward a soft affirmation. He feels he has grown from the relationship, even from the break-up. This case example is the sense in which we perceive the continuum by this simple straight line diagram:

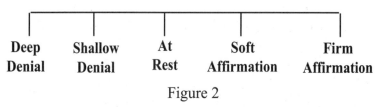

| Deep Denial | Shallow Denial | At Rest | Soft Affirmation | Firm Affirmation |

Figure 2

Absurdities may fall anywhere on this line. Obviously those falling closer to firm affirmation tend to generate more positive feelings; happy, peaceful, spirited, ambitious, loving, hopeful, vigorous. Those falling in the denial realm generate more negative feelings; sadness, laziness, anger, depression, panic, compulsion, hopelessness.

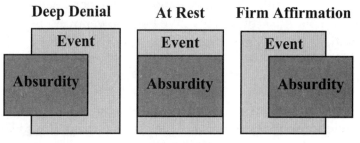

Figure 3

Since our absurdities can change, the direction of their change can strongly influence our feelings. Moving toward the left will tend to deflate the feeling, even if it started out strongly affirming. Similarly, moving toward the right can brighten the feeling even if started out deep in the denial range.

We have the capacity to reevaluate the significance we have given events in our life. Another example is a personal friend who was devastated many years ago by not making his college basketball team, after being the first string point guard on his high school team. He soon reevaluated the rejection, joined the drama club and has been a successful avocational actor for forty years.

We can also give more affirming significance to future events in our life, even those that seem to be adversities at first glance. For example, I have a dentist appointment next week. "Oh, the pain. The novocaine needle always hurts me. Then half my mouth is dead for hours...can't even drink coffee afterwards for fear it will burn my tongue. That awful tingle when the novocaine wears off. My lip itches for hours. Ugh!"

"Now wait a minute. That tooth has been hurting for weeks. It's sensitive to cold...haven't been able to eat or drink anything cold for what seems like forever. I can't chew on that side and that's the side where I usually chew. All that will be relieved. For just a little discomfort, I'll be back to normal with a healthy mouth again. It's worth it. Bring on the dentist!" Since we create our absurdities, we can have them "shift right," thus lessening our denial and pain, enhancing our life affirmations. We have power over our absurdities. It's silly not to use this power to our gain.

RECAP

Our absurdities are the significance we give to events in our lives. We are their creator. The reason they are absurd is because there are no universal meanings, no ultimate significances that are "writ in the stars." There are only your meanings and my meanings. We each define the universe by our own absurdities. Since your meanings are often different from mine, yours seem absurd to me. However, I must face the likelihood that mine are absurd as well.

My absurdities can help me get to where I want to go in life, or they can hold me back. They can range from highly affirming to deeply denying.

I also create my own feelings that can range from ultimate joy to profound despair. My feelings are almost always generated by my absurdities and since I can change my absurdities I can change my feelings. Bottom line is that I have considerable control over what is meaningful to me and the feelings I want to have. I can make myself content...and I can make myself miserable. At one time or another most of us have probably done both.

AND NEXT

Although we create our absurdities, sometimes they get mislaid...like those damnable car keys. It is difficult on occasion to identify our absurdities, especially those we formed in earlier years. And when we do find them, they seem to be mired in their original position...resistive to alteration. In the segments that follow we talk about where our absurdities come from in the first place; how we can identify our absurdities, how we can ferret out our more illusive absurdities, focusing on the ones that are giving us trouble; how can we tweak them, or bend the troublesome ones to our affirming advantage?

Meaning

Event → Absurdity → Feeling

CHAPTER 3

THE BIRTHPLACE OF OUR ABSURDITIES
WHY DO WE BELIEVE WHAT WE BELIEVE IN THE FIRST PLACE?

"We are what we think. All that we are arises with our thoughts. With our thoughts we make the world."

- Dhammapada 1

ARE MY ABSURDITIES MY OWN?

We have said before that we write our own absurdities and are free to change the script.

We meet someone. Their first impression upon us forms our initial absurdity. As we have additional experiences with that person, our absurdity may be fortified or it might change - very often the latter, again and again, until a certain stability is reached, and even then an incident might easily come along that throws that absurdity into a cocked hat once more.

But where do our absurdities come from? How do we come to believe what we believe? Your authors believe that most of our absurdities come from three sources, with a fourth that may not be a source of absurdities, but a strong influence on the significance we give to things.

FROM OTHERS

Many of our absurdities are suggested or urged upon us by other people. Those responsible for our upbringing bombard us with our earliest absurdities.

We are remanded over and over again to cross the street at a corner where there's a stop-light and to wait for the light to be favorable for crossing. One of us was raised in a city where this caution was driven into me over and over until at last on my very own, with no cautioning from anyone, I went to a corner, waited for the light to change, and then crossed. At that moment I took over the ownership of that absurdity. It was mine. It was urged by others - I remember that alright - but it wasn't my own absurdity until I took it into myself. For what it's worth, that absurdity did not last too long without alteration. I am notorious for crossing streets today opportunistically. I see an opening in the middle of the block...in a flash I cross. What? Waste half my life waiting for a light to change? Never! A perfect example of an absurdity initially impressed by others...then adopted as my own...then later altered by own volition...pretty much discarded actually, unless I'm walking down a street with my young grandson, in which event I resurrect the original absurdity to the letter.

Yes, one of us was raised as a liberal New York Democrat. I have voted for a few Republicans in my day, but when in doubt, my fall-back position is still the Democratic ticket. The other of us was raised in a comparatively conservative smaller town environment. Both of us have come to our current beliefs (absurdities), which are much more flexible and varied than our upbringings, through a gradual process of altering our early absurdities.

Many of our absurdities are adopted from other people, but they are not OUR absurdities until we take them as our own - incorporate them in our viscera, so to speak, such as the absurdities we have accepted from our school teachers. We are taught many things that form the basis of our later lives, but only the teachings we took in as our own are of significance to us. The others have wafted into the ether. Some teachings are deep within us, a part of our core beliefs. Others are floating at the edge of our significance...still a part of our belief system, but not as central, not as influential upon later absurdities we may take in as our own.

Throughout our lives other people may influence the absurdities we accept as our own. Spouses and partners influence us. Bosses, fellow workers, friends, enemies, editorial writers, strangers, fictional heros, movie characters, comic strip animals may shape our absurdities. As much as we hate to admit it, even the politician plants a notion or two - the grandest absurdity of them all!

We make no value judgment here. Some of the absurdities we accept through the influence of others serve us well...and some not so well. Suffice it to say others influence our absurdities, but none of these absurdities are indelible. Some are rewritten before the ink is dry. THEY ARE NOT IMMUNE TO CHANGE. Some of the absurdities we take in as children have been around a long time and may be a bit more difficult to uncover and mutate than later absurdities...but we can still change them. We write the script and we edit it every day of our lives.

FROM OUR OWN MIND

Most of our absurdities come from our own evaluation of the events in our lives. We assign our own significance to things, our own absurdities. Sometimes this process is very subtle; an absurdity slips into us hardly noticed. One of us is a car person. I can drive by an automobile showroom and some feature of a new car model will slip into my significance; the new Audi has an unusually tucked under quality to its front end! This absurdity slips into me almost without my knowing it. The absurdities that we take into ourselves come in mostly unnoticed unless they are reasonably close to one end or the other of the above denial-affirmation scale.

On the other hand, we trumpet in some of our absurdities...nothing subtle about it. Many people come back from seeing the Toronto theatre version of "Phantom of the Opera" saying it was the most thrilling stage performance they have ever seen. The significance they have given that performance will remain prominent for them for many

years. On the disaffirming scale, someone might be so negatively affected by the death of a person close to them, they
enter a deep depression that they think will last forever.

Once again, we write the scenario of our absurdities.

FROM DREAMS

Some of our absurdities originate in dreams, and dreams
will sometimes pull up absurdities that have become obscure
to us when we're awake. Many of our dreams evoke strong
feelings, which almost always emanate from one or another
of our absurdities. Occasionally an absurdity, usually an early
one, evokes such deep negative feelings that we take on other
absurdities to surround or otherwise protect us from having
to deal with the deeply negative one. We call these "guardian absurdities." Our dreams will sometimes let us get
through the guardians to see the "deep denial" absurdity. This
may have the appearance of originating an absurdity, when
it is actually exposing a very old one. In our view, dreams
are mostly the exposure or magnification of existing absurdities that may be illusive in the waking state, with an em-
phasis, sometimes dramatic, on their attendant feelings.
Dreams occasionally hint to a revision of an absurdity that
might moderate strong negative feelings. Least frequently,
a new absurdity originates in a dream. The point is that even
in our sleep we are the masters of our absurdities.

ABSURDITIES INFLUENCE ABSURDITIES

Perhaps one of the strongest influences upon the absurdities we accept into ourselves is the collective influence of
our previous absurdities. If I am a staunch Democrat (a previous absurdity) and I am introduced to a Republican candi-
date, my initial absurdity about him or her will likely result
in a cautious rejection. That may not last, but my initial
impression will likely be influenced by my previous absurdities. As counselors, we have had clients who had strong

negative absurdities about people of the opposite gender. It is difficult for them to meet a person of that gender (even a therapist) without an initial negative spin.

As a general observation, the more an absurdity is all-encompassing, the more restricting it actually becomes. It preconditions a person to accept absurdities that are like the all-encompassing one and to reject absurdities that may vary even slightly. If I have accepted the absurdity that all therapists are into their trade only for the money, it will be difficult for me to meet any therapist without putting a hand on my wallet. In the authors collective counseling experiences, it is these widely overgeneralized absurdities that lock a person into a narrow absurdity pattern, freeze out diversified absurdities, and often block people from their life goals and affirming feelings. We will come back to this notion in a later section.

COMPOSITE

We each create our own absurdities mostly from events that take place in our lives, or that might take place at some future time. Some of our absurdities are influenced by other people: the people who raised us as children, our teachers, our friends and adversaries, our spouses or partners, our workplace contacts, even fictional characters - BUT - they are not our absurdities until we internalize them as our own. Dreams are more often a way of revealing and dramatizing existing absurdities than a source of absurdity creation. Our existing absurdities can influence or give a bias to our newer absurdities which can narrow the expanse of our absurdities in general, or limit the significance we give to our life experiences.

CHAPTER 4

<hr>

LOST AND FOUND: HIDING OUR PAINFUL ABSURDITIES
HOW CAN WE FIND THOSE BELIEFS WE BURY LIKE DOG BONES?

Cogito, ergo sum (I think, therefore I am)
- Rene Descartes

I CREATED MY ABSURDITIES; HOW CAN THEY BE LOST?

If I am the author of my own absurdities, the significance I put on the events in my life, how can I lose them? Easily! If I make a model airplane, I might put it someplace and then forget where I put it. This may be unlikely in the case of one model, but if I make thousands of airplane models, it is not only possible, but even likely I will misplace some of them. If I make some model airplanes that I don't like, that look ugly to me, with parts in wrong places, I'll make sure I put them someplace where I won't find them, like a trash can out in the garage.

So it is with our beliefs, our absurdities. Some we use every day and are always at our fingertips. Some we use less frequently and file appropriately, like "aunt Martha is a consummate fabricator" is filed under "aunt," and maybe cross-referenced under "fabricator."

Some of our beliefs give rise to such painful feelings - (my father came into my room one night, pulled back the covers and...) - that we file them in a locked vault and scramble the combination in our mind. We may even surround the vault with guardian absurdities to make sure we won't ever have to face that vault again!

We are as capable of hiding our absurdities as we are of placing them prominently for easy access. In general terms, we have active files for frequent use, such as "it's important for me to get to work every day". We have files for less active use, such as "I don't like it, but everyone should file an annual tax return". And then we have those hidden vaults for such an absurdity as "I might have rescued my best platoon buddy who was shot down in a field in Nam, but I was too scared".

BEYOND QUESTION

Perhaps the most prevalent block to identifying an absurdity is the notion that a belief is beyond questioning...it is an untouchable truth. It is filed in a drawer labeled "Not To Be Examined" or "Beyond Refute." The person who believes that most beliefs are beyond self- examination is often the person who has most difficulty identifying beliefs when something in life is causing pain, discomfort, dysfunction or disorientation. As we indicated previously, if all our beliefs were beyond refute, and some of them were giving rise to negative feelings, we would be stuck with those negative feelings forever.

Clearly the first step in identifying a belief or an absurdity is to recognize that beliefs are not beyond questioning. As a human being I can THINK ABOUT MY THINKING, or I can abdicate that capacity by believing my beliefs are beyond doubting.

Some scholars say the expression by Rene Descartes used to introduce this chapter is more accurately interpreted not as "I think therefore I am," - but - "I DOUBT therefore I am." Questioning is considered the highest form of thinking.

This is why in writing this book, we call our beliefs ABSURDITIES. The notion of BELIEF carries a connotation of certainty, conviction, creed, dogma, the Rock of Gibraltar. ABSURDITY, on the other hand opens up its arms, declaring to self, others and the universe, "QUESTION ME...I AM NOT BEYOND DOUBT."

We have coined the term "reflective judgment" as this ability to open ourselves up for questioning. Without a willingness for reflective judgment, we have little chance to run down the absurdities spawning our discomfort, no less bending them to our advantage. Are we willing to take a seat in the witness chair of our mind and subject ourselves to self-questioning - even cross examination if need be?

WHICH ABSURDITIES TO IDENTIFY

We suspect that no one, or hardly anyone, can identify all of their absurdities, or would want to, or would have cause to do so. We've got them stored up by the thousands. Primarily, it is not the affirming absurdities, but the ones that are denying our affirmation - causing us pain - that we may want to identify and isolate for examination.

Let us examine an absurdity that generates discomfort. That discomfort is made even more intense when it bumps up against an earlier belief that was not a source of any negative feeling. A woman is pregnant in a circumstance that for her is most discomforting. Perhaps the man has left the scene; she has no means of support for a child; her health is generally poor; she has no desire for motherhood. Her belief (absurdity) is that she must not bring this child into the world...she must abort the pregnancy. She feels miserable, anxious, depressed, frightened, confused. This absurdity also is in conflict with an earlier belief that all forms of life, especially human life, are precious and should be preserved. She is a "right to life" advocate. This conflict of absurdities elevates her negative feelings, even to the brink of hopelessness.

Obviously she needs to call up the earlier belief and clearly identify it. Once she has done that, she may affirm that belief and continue the pregnancy. She may discard it and terminate the pregnancy. She may find some way to

bend the absurdity to terminate the pregnancy without dis-
carding the belief entirely - after all the doctor says things
are not developing normally; this may be a unique circumstance. Changing absurdities is discussed in later chapters,
but an obvious prerequisite is to identify the absurdities, past,
current, even future, as a preparation for their reexamination.

We need to identify those absurdities that are in, or moving toward, the denial end of the denial - affirmation continuum. We also need to identify earlier beliefs that are in
conflict with a current absurdity. These are the ones that need
modifying to return us to what we have called Firm Affirmation. We have knowingly used a most controversial issue as
our example here, not to resolve the issue, but to exemplify
the delicacy, yet importance of the absurdity identification
process. As you know, we feel there are NO UNIVERSAL
MEANINGS. The significance we give to the concept of life
is our personal belief which is obviously an absurdity because we know it is not UNIVERSALLY shared. Recognizing that our beliefs are not TRUTHS FOR ALL HUMAN-
ITY helps us to identify our own beliefs, especially when
they clash with later experiences and beliefs. This humbles
us - makes us unpretentious - to lay bare our absurdities for
our own scrutiny; a necessary step toward resolving our inner conflicts.

A word needs to be said here, as we contemplate our
discomforting absurdities, not to underestimate the power of
our affirming absurdities. In fact, we are accessing one or
another of our affirming absurdities all the time as a part of
the self-affirmation process. This calling upon affirmations
is less dramatic to us because of the absence of negative feelings, but affirmations are the springboards of our contentment.

Life is fraught with changes and choices. If we staunchly
refuse to re-examine the significance we have put on things,
re-examine our absurdities, the journey is often made tedious
and tortuous. We have then locked ourselves into a cell of
our own making.

CATEGORIES OF ABSURDITIES

At times we can identify an illusive absurdity by focusing on beliefs that can be grouped by a common characteristic. The time frame covered by the absurdity might be such a common characteristic. Is it a belief about some past occurrence - something that is occurring now - something that might occur in the future - something I might imagine occurring? Once I have uncovered the category, I can begin to focus on the particular absurdity. Some of the more common groupings of absurdities are related below.

ABSURDITY CLUSTERS

Some absurdities exist in isolation, but most do not. Absurdities are frequently clustered around a common event or subject. Returning to my aunt Martha, the consummate fabricator... well, she is also the life of the party, especially when she embellishes the things she imagines happened to her...BUT...don't lend her any money, you'll never get a cent of it back! These are three absurdities about aunt Martha, my personal beliefs about her. I probably have a half dozen more! Multiple beliefs on a common theme (absurdity clusters) enrich the fabric of aunt Martha.

The person who is significantly depressed might think or say "I can't do anything right." "Nobody knows if I'm even in the room." "I'm a wet blanket." "I take the smile off other people's faces." The cumulative effect of this cluster of absurdities, all of them negative, chisels a distinct sculpture of the depression.

If we latch on to one absurdity about something, we can look for other absurdities about that same thing. This deepens the significance, the attendant value of the circumstance.

SELF, OTHERS, THINGS

We often categorize absurdities by 1) those pertaining to self, like the depressed person; 2) those pertaining to other

people or another person, like dear aunt Martha's agile fab-
rications; 3) those pertaining to anything other than self or
other people, like kiwifruit is a poor excuse for a fruit.
Whether the absurdity is about self, other or thing, it is still
MY absurdity. It is inside me - it is my belief about self,
other or kiwifruit.

Of course, an absurdity may be any combination of self,
other or thing. I am an inferior human being when it comes
to climbing mountains - is a combination of self and thing.
My spouse's constant nagging gets me so angry I can't see
straight - is a combination of other and self. When it comes
to handling money and balancing the books, my business
partner is a genius compared to my incompetency - has ele-
ments of all three.

This categorization of absurdities can be a powerful aid
when reaching for an illusive, yet troubling absurdity. Is it
an absurdity about myself that is causing me such discomfort? Is it in relationship to another person, other people,
society? Is it an event, an object, something happening in
the world that bothers me so?

THE MIND'S PROPENSITY FOR DUALITY

Many students of how the mind works talk of the human propensity for duality, to think in "this and that" terms:
good and evil, black and white, time and space, here and
there, finite and infinite, I and thou, inner and outer, body
and mind, perfect and imperfect, sacred and profane, spiri-
tual and material, subjective and objective. A key duality is
the notion of something in a class of things as distinct from
all other things in that class: red and all colors not red, Asian
and all races not Asian, simple and all other degrees of difficulty. This is a way our mind can take multiple gradations
of things and reduce them to the lowest multiple: two.

This propensity for duality can be helpful in the search
for illusive absurdities, particularly those that are most disturbing to us: find out what is disturbing from all things that

are not disturbing. For example, I was working with an extremely anxious person who presented that she had just about a perfect relationship with everyone in her immediate family. No significant glitches. Mother, father, husband, siblings, grandparents, uncles, aunts had all been wonderful during her thirty-two years of life. We went on a gradual search for hints of imperfection. It didn't take long to find a few, including a close relative who sexually invaded her for many early years...and another relative who reined her in so tightly, especially during adolescence, there had been little opportunity for her to find her own way in the world. With a little urging she was able to question this belief that everything was fine with everyone (a guardian absurdity) - by searching for what might not have been fine with someone. She soon found some blatant "un-fines."

The inner and outer, self and other, dualities are particularly ripe for finding illusive and troubling beliefs (absurdities). A person who carries excessive hostility toward another person or other people in general, may be inviting an inner look at a self-disturbance to uncover the enraging root.

A hunt for duality is often a path to reveal some of our most disturbing beliefs. Many therapists have been using "paradox" for years to work especially on phobic and obsessive situations. We will explore more on this later, but suffice it for now to suggest that paradox is an extension of the duality notion, like something that appears written in tiny, unreadable letters on a deflated balloon, then becomes clearly pronounced in capital letters when that balloon is inflated.

PEELING THE ABSURDITY

This categorization is like the previously discussed clusters of absurdities around a common theme, except the multiple absurdities are in a sense, arranged in layers. It is like scratching under an absurdity to find another, and then possibly another, getting closer to a central or perhaps core absurdity. Here, again, this layering most often takes place with absurdities that are in the denial range, usually engendering disquieting feelings deepening to displeasure, discomfort, arousal and often self-abasement.

In absurdity therapy, we call this "peeling the absurdity" - taking off the outer peel, often to see a second peel, removing it, to see yet another peel, until we reach what the peels are encircling...a central stuff or combination of stuffs. Other metaphors could be used, but we prefer "peeling" - which most people can do for themselves. As an example, we look at the peeling done by a person who, without warning, is let go from his or her job:

OUTER PEEL: "They had no right to fire me after twelve and a half years." - This is the peel, or outer absurdity that might be expressed to a spouse, close relatives, friends and fellow workers. The absurdity is an indignation at a very unjust circumstance, but it doesn't end there. We peel off the outer layer?

NEXT PEEL: "All those years I felt I was doing a good job; no reprimands, pay increases every couple of years, a letter of commendation, longer vacations." This peeling reveals twelve and half years of affirmations. An uplifting absurdity that affirms that they knew I was good...so did I. But what is the peel under that?

NEXT PEEL: "Now, all of a sudden, they think I'm no good. Just out the door - with pocket change for separation pay. The bastards." Yes, anger and disappointment show at this peel...and rejection, but it's rejection outside of myself, their rejection of me. It may be difficult to peel off this layer, but there is a sense of another layer...a kind of fear.

NEXT PEEL: "I'm in my fifties now. Lots of smart kids out there looking for work. Mine was a specialty job - not many of them around any more." The rejection has taken an inward turn. This is a future oriented absurdity of personal rejection, accompanied probably by fear and the gnawing apprehension of lesser opportunity - a diminishment of comforts...the ravages of age. This was indeed a difficult peel, but the peels are getting thinner now, almost visible underneath each other.

NEXT PEEL: "O my God, my youngest kid may not be able to go to college. I'll have to draw on savings I wanted to preserve. I'll have to cancel vacation plans. I can't contribute to my retirement any more." A flooding is in process now; flooding myself with the consequences of my self-rejection. Apprehension escalates to anxiety. Fear and anger are displaced by depression.

THE CORE: What good am I? I failed. What a worthless human being I am!

Almost all psychotherapies recognize this process and name it differently. The psychoanalysts speak of repression and repressed memories. The cognitive therapists speak of underlying automatic thoughts, which the rational-emotive-behavioral adherents call evaluative thoughts. We call it peeling the absurdity because at the core, surrounded by outer peels of absurdities, is usually one of the prima-absurdities...in this case a personal worthlessness. The core absurdity is often the most obvious in having NO UNIVERSAL MEANING. The core absurdity often fulfills the more common definition of absurd: unsound, incongruous, unprovable, and ridiculously unreasonable. It's so clear. If I can declare myself unworthy, I can declare myself worthy just like that. I can declare my worthiness is not an issue here; I'm leaving it to Buddha, or another wise one. How absurd. How absurd. The wing is on the bird!

COGITO ERGO SUM-MATION

We are capable of misplacing some of our absurdities, especially those that cause us grief and carry us away from where we would like to go in life. To identify our beliefs we must first ready ourselves for self reflection, to question ourselves, to employ one of the human mind's finest capacities: doubt. We often have no difficulty doubting others, so we know the process...we just need to configure it to ourselves.

It helps to recognize there are categories of beliefs. We usually have clusters of absurdities around a common theme as opposed to a single belief about something. Our beliefs are commonly about ourselves - others - things - or combinations of these three. Our mind tends to think or categorize in dualities and knowing this can help identify illusive beliefs.

Some of our absurdities surround a core absurdity and need to be peeled off to get to the central belief, which is often the most absurd of all.

Again, we need to identify those absurdities that most deny, or work against our firm affirmations. Once we identify the absurdity, we can change it. We can alter it to remove the discomfort or negative feeling it is spawning in us. We can "shift it to the right" toward where we want to go. It is to this absurdity metamorphosis that we now turn.

CHAPTER 5

THE ART OF DEFUSING
A PAINFUL ABSURDITY
WE CAN ALTER A BELIEF
WITH THE FLICK OF THE MIND

The mind is its own place and in itself can make a heav'n of hell, a hell of heav'n.
> - John Milton from <u>Paradise Lost</u>.

You can't keep the birds of sorrow from flying over your head, but you can keep them from building nests in your hair.
> - Chinese Proverb (undated)

BELIEFS ARE FOR THE CHANGING

To change an absurdity that is causing a discomforting feeling first requires acceptance that our beliefs are susceptible to change. As the poet Milton suggests, our mind can exalt what damns us and dampen what exalts us. This is a reasonable corollary of the notion in the previous chapter that to identify an illusive absurdity we must accept the concept of doubt or self-questioning. The process of change first asks the question - now that I've uncovered the bloody absurdity, do I believe I can tweak it? Can I believe the significance I have put on something is all wet, or at least damp?

As mentioned earlier, we change our beliefs all the time. I heard a piece of music on the radio a few weeks ago that I found startling and stirring. It had me moving my body in a kind of dance while I was sitting in a chair. I bought the CD so I could listen to it at my leisure...over and over. With about the seventh playing I started thinking differently about it. It seemed raucous and atonal to me. The disjointed cadence of it actually started to irritate me, an incessant cacophony that just wouldn't let up. The significance I have given this piece of music has done a virtual one-eighty. Perhaps if I file the CD in some remote place, I may pull it out in a year or two and enjoy it again. This is a rather simplistic example of changing a belief, but it demonstrates it can be done. We do it all the time.

The first step is accepting that a belief - yes, one of my own precious beliefs - may be erroneous. In the case of this musical selection the defects became quite obvious and obnoxious to me. The music started to affect my viscera differently. What had at first stirred me, in the sense of exciting my musical curiosity, began to stir me discordantly, almost nauseously. Changing the absurdity then came easily.

Unfortunately, this is not always so simple. When an absurdity is deeply troubling us, we can become fixated, like a needle stuck in the groove of a phonograph record (remember them?), playing itself again and again, gradually digging the groove deeper and deeper. Then, the troubling emotion spawned by the absurdity, such as anxiety or depression, becomes so intense we can no longer focus on the absurdity or on escaping the groove it is in.

This "Catch-22" is how we lose contact with absurdities. We have a belief, or cluster of absurdities that stir up a discomforting feeling. As the absurdity entrenches, the feelings get stronger. As the feelings deepen or intensify, our ability to focus (keep a clear picture of our thoughts) becomes blurred. As we go further out of focus we lose the ability to identify the absurdity that gave rise to the discomfort in the first place. WE ARE STUCK.

We need to identify and change the absurdity in order to modify the disturbing feeling or the errant behavior...BUT...we are too upset to identify the absurdity...PLUS...if we do identify the absurdity, it is so entrenched we have trouble believing it can be FLAWED or that it can be changed. Thus WE ARE STUCK with the unwanted feeling; fear, depression, anxiety, obsession, anger, whatever. There is a circularity to this process, the head obscuring the tail that whipped the head!

A DRIVING EXAMPLE

On a lighter side, both authors have had the experience of driving a car in England, where, as is generally known to Americans, they drive on the wrong side of the road. They even put the steering wheel on the wrong side of the car!

Not generally known are the "round-abouts" they have everywhere in England, not only for city streets but for country lanes as well: many roads converging from various directions into a circle that you must go at least partially around to continue your journey. Now, doing one of these round-abouts going in the wrong counter-clockwise direction on the wrong side of the road while driving from the wrong side of the car and having to exit on the wrong side of your exit way is about as disorienting as can be imagined. Even experienced Brits have been known to pass where they came into the circle once or twice before getting to where they want to get off. A non-Brit like me can get dizzy going around so many times and the chances are incredibly high that I will exit on the wrong side of the wrong road and I won't know it until I run into either 1) another car, 2) the English channel or 3) the Irish Sea!

Please accept this as metaphor for going in circles to find the absurdity that gets you out of a painful, detouring feeling and back on the road that takes you where you want to go in life.

FLAWED

Once you have found the absurdity generating the painful feelings, the first step in changing the absurdity is to ac-

cept that it may be flawed. This is not always an easy acceptance. The absurdity engendering the most pain may appear
deeply imbedded and seemingly flawless. The "peeling"
example in the previous chapter found the core absurdity of
the person who lost his job was "I am a worthless human
being." Although it may be obvious to others that this is a
flawed belief - a most conspicuous absurdity - it is common
for a person who feels unworthy and without esteem to think
that's an unalterable, immutable truth.

Similarly, a person who is depressed because he or she
thinks "I'm a loser. I'll never succeed" - is often stuck in
that belief, conceiving it as unchangeable. An anxious, wor-
ried person may be self-righteously locked into the conviction "If I fail it would be terrible."

The first step is to recognize that any of our beliefs - our
absurdities - may be flawed. Those absurdities that are causing us discomforting feelings or counter-productive behaviors, keeping us from our Firm Affirmations, are obviously
flawed. They are making us miserable in one way or another, moving toward Deep Denial which is our definition
of "flawed." In later chapters we will review some of the
absurdities that frequently accompany particularly upsetting
feelings and behaviors. They are all flawed absurdities.
Why? Because they are upsetting. If they were not flawed,
they would be calming or affirming. This concept seems so
obvious, it must obviously be absurd!

We acknowledge here that not all discomforting feelings are counter-productive or inappropriate. As discussed
in the previous chapter, the mind's propensity for duality
suggests we need some discomforting feelings to identify
contrast; unhappiness to enable us to have some gauge of
happiness. Anxiety may be appropriate to draw someone's
attention to a dangerous or threatening situation. Anger is
sometimes needed to focus our energy and concentration on
a challenging task. Sadness is often a necessary feeling in
getting through a difficult loss.

Discomforting feelings are a part of the living process...actually needed at times to guide our appropriate behaviors...to help us move forward to where we want to go. Few paths in life are without detours and side roads to help us know the desired path...or to help us find new paths, even more affirming. Discomforting feelings can be part of growth and personal development. It is like the seemingly endless agony of constant practice needed to master the violin, or becoming a lawyer, or losing unwanted weight. We make the distinction here - not always easy - between discomfort needed to recognize or achieve comfort, and unnecessary discomfort that does little but generate unwanted feelings and act as quicksand on the life journey.

RECORDING AND GRADING

Let's assume for the moment I have uncovered an absurdity that is generating considerable discomfort in me. Any and all of the techniques for identifying an absurdity as discussed in the previous chapter are available to me. Chances are it is not a single absurdity, but a cluster of absurdities, or layering of absurdities as reviewed earlier. We may not see any flaw in the beliefs - they seem to us to be self-evident truths. But whenever I let myself focus on the beliefs, I can feel the pain or discomfort. The anger churns up in me; or I feel myself shrinking into a shell; or I can sense the anxiety building, even foretelling a panic attack. Whenever this happens we ASSUME the absurdity is flawed, even though we may not completely accept that at this point. We might liken the closeness of an absurdity and the feeling it generates to an item of food and the way that food tastes. If the taste is unpalatable, there is probably something wrong with the food.

The first step is to capture the absurdity, write it down or speak it into a tape recorder AND immediately thereafter write or record the discomforting feelings that accompany that belief. Figure 4 is a form for capturing the event, the absurdity and the feelings that accompany that absurdity, if you chose to put it in writing. The other option is to read each question into a tape recorder and record your response. Some people are quite comfortable writing things down, in fact it helps clarify what their beliefs and feelings are at any point in time. Others are more verbal in the way they prefer to process this information; they prefer not to write things

THE EVENT - THE ABSURDITY - THE FEELING - THE BEHAVIOR

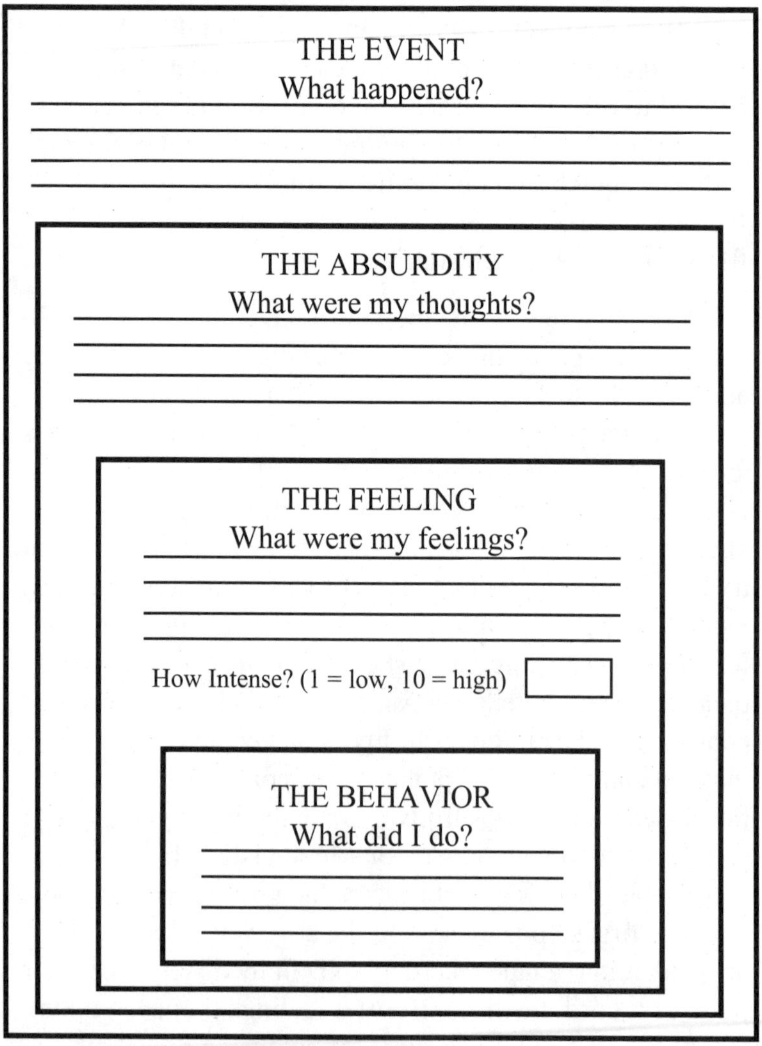

THE EVENT
What happened?

THE ABSURDITY
What were my thoughts?

THE FEELING
What were my feelings?

How Intense? (1 = low, 10 = high)

THE BEHAVIOR
What did I do?

Figure 4

down, but to speak them out...and in this case it is important to capture these beliefs and feelings on tape so they can be re-experienced. From our experience, there are some advantages in writing it down, usually quicker, easier to review and more easily accessed at a later time. When writing things down, we suggest a minimum of words. Lengthy explanations are not needed, in fact they can be counter-productive. You just need a few words to bring the event, absurdity and feelings back into recollection. This is why we don't make room for lots of writing on most of the forms we use.

Use one form for each absurdity, or a separate recording for each absurdity as if you were using a separate form. Don't put multiple absurdities together. The object is to recognize that each of these absurdities generating the discomforting feeling is most likely FLAWED.

We also suggest grading the intensity of the feeling from one to ten, with one being not at all intense, more like a twinge; ten is very intense, almost overwhelming for quite awhile; five would be distinctly discomforting, but not overwhelming.

If this feeling leads to your reacting to the feeling, that is, doing something because of it, we suggest you also record this reaction, or what we call the RESULTING BEHAVIOR (discussed below).

The following examples are from actual situations reported to us.

EVENT: Eating alone in a restaurant. The waitress threw the check down on the table and immediately turned away. ABSURDITY: She has no time for me. Probably dislikes me. FEELINGS: Anger at first, then self doubt, loneliness, depression. INTENSITY: 7. RESULTING BEHAVIOR: I quickly paid and left the restaurant leaving just a small tip.

EVENT: A car cut in front of me, making me brake to avoid hitting him. ABSURDITY: Stupid jerk...how could he drive so stupidly. FEELING: Anger, damn near rage. IN-

TENSITY: 10. RESULTING BEHAVIOR: I later pulled up beside him, gave him the finger.

EVENT: My ten year old son told me he hated me. ABSURDITY: He has no respect for me. I'm a lousy mother. FEELING: Hurt, rejected, depressed. INTENSITY: 9. RESULTING BEHAVIOR: I walked into another room and started crying.

EVENT: I lost sight of a woman who came food shopping with me. ABSURDITY: I've lost her. I'm alone here. I'm trapped in the store and can't get out. FEELING: Frightened, anxious, panicky. INTENSITY: 8. RESULTING BEHAVIOR: I almost had a panic attack, but warded it off.

This is an important step in the process for changing an absurdity and its attendant feeling: practicing over and over to learn the linkage of beliefs and feelings, especially those beliefs that are making us miserable.

THE FEELING - BEHAVIOR CONNECTION

In each of the examples cited above, the intense discomforting feeling was accompanied by, or gave rise to, a BEHAVIOR that reflected that feeling. The absurdity that the waitress doesn't like me - which had me feeling self-doubting, lonely and depressed - resulted in my exiting the restaurant and leaving a small tip.

The absurdity that the jerk who cut in front of me could have killed me - which enraged me - resulted in my chasing him and giving him the finger.

The absurdity that I'm a lousy mother - which had me feeling hurt, rejected and depressed - resulted in my going to another room and crying.

The absurdity that I was trapped in that supermarket - which had me feeling anxious and panicky - almost caused me to have a panic attack right there in the store.

It is often the case that intense discomforting feelings give rise to behaviors that reflect that intense discomfort. This is portrayed diagrammatically, in Figure 4.

INFUSING A SERIES OF EVENTS - ABSURDITIES - FEELINGS - BEHAVIOR

What can happen then is that this BEHAVIOR which flowed from the intense discomfort of a previous absurdity, becomes the EVENT in a new, but connected series of Events - Absurdities - Feelings - Behaviors.

For example: The new Event is: I caught up with the jerk who cut in on me and gave him the finger. He rolled down his window and said "Fucketh Thou," made a quick right turn and got away from me. New Absurdity: He screwed me again. The world is full of jerks who screw you every chance they get. New Feeling: seething - an intense, pervasive anger, Intensity 10+. New Resulting Behavior: I speedily drove home, pulled a beer out of the refrig, and waited for someone to cross me.

This behavior, of course, is inviting the next new Event - Absurdity - Feeling - Behavior and so forth, all of which builds a sense of rage and burrows it deeper into my emotional core. In this example we have made everything happen quickly, one event right after the other. This chain or series of Events - Absurdities - Feelings - Behaviors can happen over a longer period of time, even with intervening absurdities on unrelated issues, but this is the process: Event > Absurdity > Feeling > Behavior > Event > Absurdity > Feeling > Behavior and so forth, as pictured in Figure 5. With a little imagination you can almost see the successive absurdities-feelings boring inward, implanting themselves into a mind-set that is difficult to escape, creating this "Well Of Disturbed Emotions" with their companion self-feeding behaviors.

SPECIFIC WAYS TO CHANGE AN ABSURDITY: THE FIRST THREE STEPS

There are several rather specific techniques for changing an absurdity, even clusters of absurdities, that we will

discuss in the ensuing chapters. Each technique pays homage to the interconnectedness of 1) events and absurdities,
the significance we give to things that happen; 2) absurdities
and feelings, knowing almost all feelings flow from what
we believe about something; 3) feelings and behaviors, recognizing that many of the things we do are spurred on by our
absurdities and feelings. There is a chain here and chances
are if we alter one point in the chain, the other points will
have to make some adjustment as well. We may not be able
to change many of the events in our lives, but we surely can
modify our beliefs, feelings and behaviors; in fact we are the
only ones who can make these modifications.

The first three steps for modifying an absurdity are the
same for all techniques: ONE; identify the absurdities that
are generating the discomforting feelings deterring us from
our Firm Affirmation, and

TWO; accept that our absurdities can be FLAWED,
especially those that are discomforting us, and

THREE, record these absurdities in some way.

From there...we move on.

The Well of Disturbed Emotions

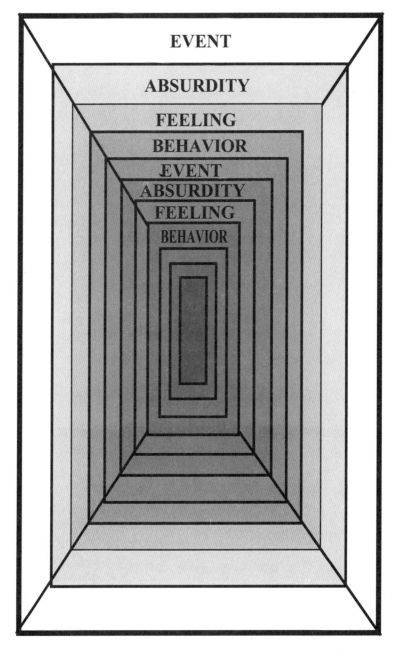

Figure 5

CHAPTER 6

---ᴐ◦◦ᴐ---

PUTTING AN ABSURDITY
ON THE WITNESS STAND
PERRY MASON-IZING A BELIEF:
PUTTING ITS FEET TO THE FIRE

Truth is the trial of itself and needs no other touch...
-Ben Jonson (1616)

ON THE WITNESS STAND

The most obvious way to change an absurdity is to take issue with it, make it prove itself, put it on the witness stand and cross examine it.

Let's go back to a previous example. The EVENT: my spouse or partner for the past ten years has left me and taken off with another person. We will assume in this case that it is a man who has run off with another woman and his wife or partner is left behind feeling miserable. The significance she has given this event, the absurdity if you will, is HOW CAN HE DO THAT? HOW CAN HE RUN AWAY AND DESERT ME...AND WITH ANOTHER WOMAN?...which reflects that her partner MUST NOT desert her. The attendant feelings are deep sorrow, anger, loneliness, despair, depression.

With these intense discomforting feelings it is not likely she will be able to confront or cross examine this absurdity right away. The feelings are too debilitating, numbing, interfering with the cognitive process. It may take a short while, living with the discomforting feelings, experiencing the pain, before she can find the absurdity and connect it to the emotional turmoil that is clearly a 10 on her feeling-intensity scale.

There is an interesting phenomena at work here. People with strong beliefs which they feel are immutable - what, me change my belief? - tend to have difficulty finding the specific absurdity that needs examining. After all, none of them need changing. On the opposite side are people who believe almost all of their beliefs are shaky to begin with. They too have difficulty identifying a specific absurdity causing pain and needing revision. After all, they all need changing.

The person with reasonably strong beliefs but who also recognizes personal beliefs are not beyond questioning, is often the quickest to identify pain-inducing absurdities and to put them on the witness stand. Their absurdities are neither cast in bronze nor built of sand. This is often the person who recognizes that although others may do things that trouble us, we are the framers of our own beliefs and feelings.

Once the absurdity is on the witness stand, the process of cross-examination can be as variable as witness examination in a real court room...depending on the ingenuity of the cross-examiner...and the presentation of contrary evidence.

THE RELATIONSHIP OF ABSURDITIES TO REALITY

We need to take a brief side road here before proceeding with our cross-examination. As we have said, we call our beliefs absurdities because there are no universal beliefs floating in space that are embraced by everyone. Our own beliefs are as absurd as we sometimes ascribe to other people's beliefs.

On the other hand there is substance and structure in the universe that is apparent to most of us, most of the time. For example, we see the same end table next to the same couch sitting on the green rug. We would pick out the same photograph of it.

Another example: when we find the newest comet in our binoculars at 10 PM just off the end of the Big Dipper as reported in the newspaper, we are all most likely seeing the same comet. It is this commonly accepted view of substance and structure that we call reality... or perceived reality, because even reality is subject to examination that can lead to a new reality. After all, it wasn't that many centuries ago when all our ancestors believed the earth was flat.

Sometimes we might have a belief, or absurdity, that runs counter to the currently accepted view of substance, structure or events. Our absurdity is in conflict with reality. This isn't always negative for us by any means. In fact, such absurdities can be delightful. A child's belief in Santa Claus is such an example, and expands the child's imagination and sense of fantasy. One of my roommates in college was Rod Serling, who later became the famed television writer and creator of "Twilight Zone."

Rod used to tell that when he was a little boy, his grandfather would take him on walks to the mailbox a mile or so away to mail a letter. Rod once asked his grandfather how they knew where to deliver the letter. His grandfather told him there was a little man in every mailbox and you had to shout to him where the letter was going...and grandpa would put a letter in the box and yell "Chicago," or wherever. Well, here many years later in college, Rod would spend one night every week writing a radio script...I know because the deal was I had to find someplace else to sleep that night. The next morning, finished script in an envelope under his arm, Serling would march to the campus mailbox, drop in the envelope, take a step back and shout "Radio City, Rockefeller Center, New York. And Hurry." (Hmmm. Was that absurdity the origin of the Twilight Zone?)

Many of our absurdities can be imaginative, not entirely lined up with the hard test of reality, and help generate good feelings and move us into creative, goal-directed behaviors. Yet the situation is quite different when we have identified an absurdity that is not positive for us, that spawns discomforting feelings and goal-defeating behaviors. Then, one of the best ways to confront that absurdity is to cross-examine it, test it against reality, by which we mean reality in the sense of commonly accepted views of substance, structure or events. This reality testing is reflected in the following cross-examination.

BACK TO THE WITNESS STAND

We return to the woman whose partner has run off with another woman and whose absurdity is "How can he can do that? How can he run away and desert me?" A cross-examination might proceed as follows:

IQ (Internal Questioner): Where is your partner now?
Self: I'm not sure. I think in Lexington, Kentucky.
IQ: And who is he with?
Self: That bitch who works with him.
IQ: How do you know?
Self: My friend, who works at the same place told me. She thought I should know.
IQ: So how can you believe "he can't do that." He HAS done it and you know it.
Self: Because he just can't. It's so unfair. I hate him for it.
IQ: Where does it say he can't. Is it written on a tablet on a mountain top. The eleventh commandment: "My partner shall not leave me for another?"
Self: No, of course not. I know it's physically possible for him to leave me. It's just so unfair. He shouldn't have done it.
IQ: But he has. From his point of view why shouldn't he. He has choices and he chose to run off with "her," however stupid it may have been from your point of view. Forget what he should or shouldn't do. What do you think and feel for yourself?
Self: I think he was very unfair to me. He betrayed me, that's what I think. It's hard to accept a loss, especially when I didn't want it to happen. I feel really sad.
IQ: As miserable as when you were saying to yourself, HE CAN'T DO THAT?
Self: Not quite that miserable, but I still feel hurt. I'm angry and I feel deserted; stabbed in the back. Sad!

In this particular case, the partner made a permenant change in his life circumstances. He called a few days later to arrange to pick up his belongings, but other than that the man just walked out of her life. Her cross-examination took a different turn sometime later:

> **IQ**: Gone is gone. I know you're still wounded, but is there anything positive about it all?
>
> **Self**: I guess. I know how important trust is to me in a relationship.
>
> **IQ**: Will this incident destroy your exploring new relationships?
>
> **Self**: I would hope not. I might move a bit more slowly to be surer that trust is building. Trust is important to me. But I'll not isolate myself.
>
> **IQ**: How does this new belief, this new absurdity, make you feel?
>
> **Self**: It's okay...I'm not ecstatic about it, but it's definitely on the positive side.

Thus the cross-examination of "He can't do that" which made her feel miserable and limited her activity, changed in steps to the absurdity, "he was unfair to me, but I learned how important trust is to me and I'll improve my search for it in future relationships," which made her feel sufficiently positive to get on with her life.

Once again we return to the ever recurrent theme of Absurdity Therapy. We are in charge of the significance we put on the events in our life. If we give something a significance that discomforts us, we can "bloody well change it." This may seem simplistic - and admittedly the process of changing an absurdity is not always so easy - but we can make it uncomplicated MOST of the time. We get through life more happily through our design, or redesign, of absurdities in a way that minimizes our pain and maximizes our sense of being okay.

COMMON CROSS-EXAMINATION QUESTIONS

The following are some of the more common cross-examination questions that often lead to a revision of the absurdity, that can soften the discomfort or even convert to positive feelings and goal-oriented behaviors.

Is The Absurdity In Tune With Reality? This is reflected in the previous inner dialogue. Absurdities out of sync with reality that are spawning painful feelings can often be moderated by reality-testing the absurdity and bringing it back into reality focus.

Sometimes reality testing an absurdity may affirm the reality, but then refocus the absurdity. A real-life example: "I must not marry this Catholic man. No one in my family accepts Catholics." The second part of this absurdity may not be at all true. We have had clients who were convinced of a common characteristic of their entire family. They were encouraged to test that reality only to find there were numerous contrary incidents. "Oh, didn't you know your uncle Charlie is Catholic...a pillar at Saint Bede's!" If the second sentence of the absurdity is false, then the essence of the belief falls apart.

On the other hand, the family characteristic may be valid, in which case you can refocus or challenge the absurdity by turning it into a question; Why must I not marry a Catholic man even though my family disfavors Catholics? This leads to a host of challenging cross-examination questions that may break down the absurdity and lead to a modification.

Is The Absurdity Expressed in Extreme Terms? Many pain-creating absurdities contain extreme expressions and words. Words like "all," "every," "everybody," "nobody," "should," "forever," "must," "never," and the like. These extreme words are particularly susceptible to cross examination. "I believe all bathroom sinks should be white." Why should they ALL be white? What's so awful about a blue one now and then? Who are you to suggest ALL of anything should be this way or that way? Many cross-examining questions could attack this notion of ALL. Most extreme beliefs are very hard to defend. Exceptions pop up everywhere. As to the meaning we each give to people, places and events, there are about as many exceptions as there are people. It is the exceptions that disprove overgeneralizations; that put the fallacy to all or nothing thinking, extreme thinking, polarized thinking, inflexible thinking

Is The Absurdity Commanding or Demanding? Very often pain inducing absurdities have a command or demand in them. This was the essence of the absurdity in the previous dialogue; He MUST NOT run away and desert me. Cross-examining the MUST is very appropriate and will often lead to soothing modifications. Words like "Must," "Can't," "Should," as so aptly pointed out by rational-emotive therapists, very often lead to inner turmoil. These words can be toned down. He MUST is softened into "he might consider or he would prefer." I CAN'T tones down to "I may not be able, or it may not be easy." I SHOULD modifies to "I may give some thought to," or "one of my possibilities is." These are softer expressions. They offer possibilities rather than giving commands. They suggest rather than demand.

A pain-inducing absurdity may often combine these two issues. They both command and use extreme terms. ALL bathroom sinks SHOULD be white. If this is my belief, it puts me in contravention with all colored sinks and in conflict with everyone who likes other than white sinks. No wonder this absurdity makes me feel miserable. I'm at war with sinks of color - and everyone who likes them! Now...to say instead, "I personally prefer white sinks and would like to see more of them" makes no demand on what sinks others prefer and acknowledges that there are some colored sinks around. That eases my pain quite a bit when I see a purple sink! I may shade my eyes, but I won't panic and I won't despair and I won't rage.

Who Does The Absurdity Command? If an absurdity is commanding, it is relevant to ask who is being commanded? There are four possibilities. The absurdity may be commanding yourself. "I must never let myself become intimate with another person."

It may command someone else. "My partner must care only for me, and that certainly excludes his play-acting-helpless mother!"

It may command society, or the world. "The whole world cheats...especially politicians and chiropractors. They must stop lying."

Lastly, it may command any combination of self - other - world. "I'm no good. You're no good and the whole world is worse than all of us put together." Now that's a pervasive negative absurdity!

CROSS EXAMINE THE ABSURDITY AGAINST THE FOUR LIFE AFFIRMING VALUES

As discussed earlier the four underlying values of a life affirming absurdity are 1) it supports our staying alive, 2) it is not in conflict with the rights of others in society, 3) it helps us achieve our personal goals, 4) it reduces the conflict in our lives, either an inner conflict with ourself or a conflict with a person or event outside of our own skin.

If an absurdity is not serving us well, leading us to hurtful feelings and unproductive behaviors, the chances are that it is rubbing against the grain of one or more of these four measures of a life affirming absurdity. Cross examining the absurdity against these values can help uncover why it is so upsetting and give us a clue for revising the absurdity to neutralize or reverse the hurt, the internal turmoil.

Let's try it with the runaway partner: HOW CAN HE DO THAT? HE MUST NOT RUN AWAY AND DESERT ME is the absurdity.

1) Is this absurdity affirming or threatening the life process? We need to cross examine it to find out.

IQ (Internal Questioner): Does his leaving make me suicidal?

Self: No. I'm not thinking of taking my life. It's not that bad. I'm just not a suicidal person.

IQ: Okay, that's not where the hurt is.

Self: Now, wait a minute. I'm not thinking suicide But my life won't be the same without him. It will never be as fulfilling. Maybe part of me is dying, taken away from me. I may never recover that part.

IQ: Just what part is that? What's your proof that it can't be recovered or replaced with something that can serve you just as well? Show me how you know what the future will bring?

This line of questioning may briefly highlight your immediate pain, but it is difficult to prove that the loss will injure you forever; that it is irreparable. This questioning often leads to some revisions in thinking like: "the pain will subside, it did with other losses, like when my good friend died." "I can't prove future misery." "Some good things can happen in my life if I don't let this incident lock me up inside." "Why should I give him power over my life or death, or the quality of my future life?" "You know, he's the one who's missing out. His life is minimized, not mine." As this kind of thinking comes into clearer focus, the absurdity begins to change, the pain softens, and in time vanishes.

2) Is this absurdity in conflict with the rights of society? Cross examination would likely establish that social codes and mores are not particularly involved with this absurdity, except for the interesting question of whether leaving a partner and taking off suddenly with another person is a social no-no. In our country it is not a violation of law. Although it is often considered a mean and unfair behavior (depending on the particular circumstances), it is a part of our societal reality. It happens with some regularity. Intimate relationships sometimes break up with one or both partners hurt in the process.

Part of the unfairness here is the absence of any considerate dialogue before the break-up, but that usually reflects more negatively upon the leaver than the person left behind. Vigorous cross examination usually has the person recognize that she is not alone. She probably knows others to whom this has occurred unfairly and who have made their way through it and moved on to satisfying lives. In fact, probably most people in their lifetime have managed to get through a requited love that became not so requited. In fact, in adolescence and young adulthood this sad experience is considered part of the expected human developmental process. Quite often these break-ups are not managed with particular grace or dignity. People often waltz into a loving relationship. The undoing may be a dance macabre!

3) It is evident this absurdity is not helping the person achieve her personal goal, which in this case is probably to have a sustaining, committed relationship. In fact the vehemence of her command that HE MUST NOT DESERT ME may so sour her on relationships...on men in general...that she may BLOCK herself from any future enduring relationship. Better not love than love and lose. Now there's an absurd absurdity for you; an elevator descending to the pits. In time she will likely come to think that he's the one having trouble with a committed relationship, not her. May this be an absurdity as well? You bet. But this absurdity does not derail the train taking her to where she wants to go!

4) The Internal Questioner hurls the inquiry; "Does this absurdity that HE MUST NOT DESERT YOU reduce the conflict in your life?"

Hardly. It generates an almost unresolvable conflict. He must not desert me...but he is in Lexington, Kentucky with the other woman and he doesn't want to come back to me...ever. This isn't just an ordinary conflict. It's a conflict with an adversary called REALITY. In time the absurdity will soften: "It's a shame. We had some good times, some rich times really. I'll be sad about us for awhile, maybe quite a while. But not bitter. Life is a river...in fact the new guy at

doesn't even know I exist.

Me? Try to swim? I'll drown.

When I can't succeed at something, it proves I'm a worthless human being.

I'm drained. I can't get anything done. I never will.

He left me. Others left me before. I'm a loser. Nobody will ever want me again.

Depression is usually a flood of self-doubt and self-downing. It is reported to be the most prevalent of the less flexible mind states. There are many reasons, of course. It's an extension of sadness. Most of us experience sadness...we almost have to as a counterpoint of joy.

Most of us experience losses in our life: through the death of someone we care for; the end of a relationship; the end of a job; the end of our youth...on and on.

I once had a psychology professor who also had an extensive private therapy practice. He lectured one day on the significance of loss as a factor of mental health.

I asked him, "With what percent of your clients is such loss a significant factor?"

He said, "At least half."

He halted me as I was leaving the classroom that day and said, "No. It's more like two-thirds."

Later that day as I was leaving the student lounge, this professor caught up with me and tapped me on the shoulder. When I turned, he just looked at me and said, "All."

With mild depression, most people can identify some of their depression-oriented absurdities using the techniques discussed earlier. This is more difficult for a severely depressed person, but with some help, he or she can uncover enough self minimizing absurdities to start the cross examination process. With some people antidepressant medication can help the person focus sufficiently to aid the absurdity searching process. Once identified, the various processes for changing, altering or tweaking an absurdity can be quite effective.

In an earlier chapter we discussed how it is virtually impossible to *prove* even the existence of worthlessness. Some self-effacing absurdities have difficulty surviving even a modest cross examination.

ABSURDITIES ASSOCIATED WITH ANGER

The key concepts here are *Demandingness and Condemnation.* Although anger is usually expressed outwardly toward others, it is just as inner-oriented as other discomforts of the less flexible mind. The message written on your forehead is "You must provide for my inner comfort." Severe and repetitive anger is a profound expression of what others should do to meet your concept of things, and because they don't, they need to be castigated. Others must conform to the working of the world as you see it. This belief or absurdity is not necessarily out of a grand conceit...in fact often quite the opposite. Needing others to see things as you see them comes more from uncertainty, a demand for affirmation, a need for others to buffer what might otherwise be a profound loneliness.

This is the way such anger often relates to loss, or more specifically the fear of loss. In working with court remanded male batterers, this fear of loss, particularly wife or partner loss, is a strong, recurring factor. The batterer may not be quick to admit it, but no matter how much he complains of his partner, he hits or intimidates her to keep alive her fear of leaving him. Most batterers claim to come from homes where father-initiated battering was persistent. Very often the woman stays in the relationship beyond any reasonable application of common sense. She, too, has become enmeshed in this often passed down battered pattern of dependency and need.

This inappropriate expression of domestic anger is very difficult to break. In the first place, it very often works. The partner takes the beating and doesn't leave...which fortifies the battering behavior.

The inappropriate expression of anger in other environments, especially the workplace, may well become ineffective, resulting in discipline, including dismissal...with little sympathy from other workers. Such anger in a social setting is often ineffective as well, losing the respect of others, including the falling off of friendships. Sometimes in a social setting, or even a work setting, the well targeted expression of even excessive anger (usually against an unpopular person) may garner some appreciation and respect, which dissuades the angered person's motivation to alter his anger oriented feelings and behavior.

Very often, however, people easy to anger are not very happy with themselves. They are uncomfortable with the persistent inner tension...the inability to relax, to feel the joy of even joyful situations. The anger comes from an insatiable absurdity: "others simply MUST give me what I want." However hard others try to do this, it is never quite enough, or it can't endure long enough. Emotional contentment dries up again and a variation of this unfulfilled absurdity must keep churning:

"You should listen to me...or obey me...or think of me...or do for me...and because you don't, you deserve to be punished, to be condemned."

"The world around me ought to give me what I want and be the way I think it ought to be."

"My partner must listen to me...yield to me."

"People should respect me; treat me kindly."

"The driver of that car had no right to cut in front of me. I must teach him (her) a lesson.

"The waitress must serve me first."

How endless are these absurdities and how constantly upsetting they must be. I am the "me of the world," but for some unfathomable reason others don't know it, or show it, or pay homage to it...thus I must constantly meter out my condemnation.

To challenge these anger generating absurdities is not easy...an act of nullifying yourself. "Who am I to suggest my way is the only way, or the best way, or even a good way? Humph, this may be easy for others to question, the myopic fools, but damnit, I know my way is beyond question." Self cross examination here takes some grit and guts. It's not easy, but in the end it is very pacifying, hushing the tumult of the mind.

As with all of the troubling feelings of a less flexible mind (anxiety, depression, anger, obsessions, stress, addictions and others) the cross examination of causal absurdities has a common impact...aiding the mind to become more *flexible*, to loosen up, to unshackle itself and *POOF*, the troubling feelings, including anger, begin to mellow. Thus challenging absurdities that espouse, declare or inflate your notion of preeminence or infallibility, is often the way to soften the tenseness, the blood rushing, the disquieting, the reddening face of anger.

ABSURDITIES ASSOCIATED WITH UNDESIRED PERFORMANCE VARIATIONS

What are some common absurdities that accompany such performance problems as overeating, under-eating, erratic sleep patterns, sexual dysfunction and the like? We are going to walk the easiest path here. We have already discussed these absurdities to a great extent.

RULING OUT A PHYSICAL PROBLEM: The first consideration is to assure that performance problems of this sort are not physiologically caused. A trip to the doctor is the first step. We are reminded of a person we knew years ago who went through lengthy unsuccessful psychotherapy for a sexual problem only to find out soon thereafter that he was diabetic and his particular physical diagnosis was also the source of his sexual problem. In almost all cases of a bodily performance problem, first get ye to a medic. To assume such problems are mental problems or thought disorders is like having a kite stuck in a tree and climbing the wrong tree to get it down!

ABSURDITIES AND BEHAVIORS NOT DIRECTLY LINKED: When a physiological problem is ruled out, it is then appropriate to embark on an absurdity hunt. HOWEVER, almost all performance problems are *behavioral* in nature. Sleep, eating, sexual anomalies are behaviors that are out of the ordinary: perhaps excessive behavior, reduced behavior, the inability to behave at all, behaving erratically or strangely. One way or another something is out of sorts with the customary way of behaving.

As we noted earlier (Chapter V to be exact) there is a flow between the events in our lives and what appear to be resulting behaviors: Event>Absurdity>Feeling>Behavior. It is the significance we give to events (our absurdities) that lead to our feelings and these feelings generate or flow into accompanying behaviors. This is a long way of saying the chances are that our diminishing sexual interest probably relates to our depression, or anxiety, or posttraumatic stress (or other feeling state). Our wanting to eat everything we can get our hands on might relate to our obsessions or compulsiveness. Our loss of appetite could well flow from feelings of depression or a diminishment of self esteem. *To find the absurdities that are leading to these behaviors, we look for the same absurdities that are generating the feeling state that spawns these behaviors.* This may sound a bit complex, but actually it's an easier search. If we tweak the absurdities of our depression, we will likely find a rekindling of our sexual ardor. Two for the price of one!

Sometimes the change in behavior is a tip off to the feeling state. I remember a woman coming in for a first counseling session. She looked a bit drawn and depressed. In presenting her problem she said, "At least I used to like sex. Now it's gone with the wind entirely." Her husband joined one or two of our sessions. Her condition began to improve. He called me about six weeks later with a kind of plea, "You think she might go for just a little depression?"

...MIND IS THE CAUSE OF LIBERATION.

We have discussed some common absurdities that often accompany various uncomfortable feelings of a less flexible mind. In discussing the absurdities that often appear with depression, anxiety, stress, anger, addiction, compulsion, and the like, we may have conveyed an overstated degree of discomfort.

We want to correct that. We are not talking just of deep or dysfunctioning depression, anxiety with agoraphobia or panic attacks, compulsions that consume several hours a day of paper folding...or other discomforts in their extreme. This linkage of absurdities applies also to much milder degrees of these discomforts. Many of us have experienced depression or anxiety that was uncomfortable but not oppressive. We have had addictions or compulsions or stresses that are painful but not disabling, but we would prefer not to have them.

These aids in absurdity identification are equally applicable to lesser levels of discomfort. In fact, absurdities can be more easily identified and altered if the discomfort is less intense and interferes less with the ability to focus. Although some of our anecdotes come from clinical practice and absurdity therapy can be a powerful clinical process, it is just as applicable, if not more so, for discomforting circumstances that do not require professional dialogue. Metaphorically, we think of absurdity therapy as over the counter, yet we would acknowledge there are cases where prescription strength (therapist assistance) is called for.

CHAPTER 9

MENDING THE MENDACITIES
THE STORY OF REGGIE

...Nought may endure but mutability.
- Percy Bysshe Shelly (1816)

IN A NUTSHELL

A primer is just that; a small introductory book. If it runs much beyond that it becomes a treatise, a book, a volume, eventually a tome. We prefer to avoid that. There is something airy about a primer. It has literary buoyancy. It doesn't ponder itself. It presents itself more than proves itself. It lays bare rather than guards or defends. It keeps its humor, discards its toil. The price is that it allows itself to be dallied about, labelled a puff, talked of in cocktail chatter. We would wish a better fate, of course, but we admit absurdity therapy is disarming in its simplicity. We are saying little more than a vigorous mind is a flexible mind, seasoned with a dash of humor. Let us wind down this primer with another story and a challenge or two.

CONSTANCY AND CHANGE

We have talked of change; that absurdity therapy is essentially mastering the art of finding and altering absurdities. But what of constancy? Was there no truth to the speech Benjamin Disraeli delivered to Parliament in 1872 (We looked it up), "The secret of success is constancy to purpose." What kind of life has no star to follow, no fundamental driving principle, no certainty of direction? Without constancy are we but wanderers, nomads in a vast desert? The case is strong for purpose in life, for without it we are but drifters in search of the unfindable.

We think we have resolved this conundrum...by joining it. Without some sense of knowing where we want to go, how can we tell we are not getting there, are slanting away from it? Absurdity therapy is dedicated to the constancy of our aims, by identifying those beliefs (absurdities) that are leading us astray. Those absurdities that are on our directional course need no tinkering. They are our oars and our compass. It is the disaffirming beliefs where we sometimes get stuck, that block us or move us away from our northern star...our focus.

Admittedly, the connection between our absurdities and our life goals may get convoluted at times. Our goals are seldom static after all. They mutate with age and circumstance. Thus, how are we to know if our absurdities are taking us to or from this shifting target.

REGGIE

I remember a dear friend of mine in high school in New York City. He was very bright. I enjoyed the agility of his mind. He saw things "differently." His father owned a six story brownstone building on Fifth Avenue where Reggie, his parents and sister lived on the top two floors. The first four floors were a medical clinic. As a highly enterprising doctor, my friend Reggie's father had an extensive and highly successful third generation medical practice, creating and running this clinic that was more like a private hospital. Reggie, the family's only son, was preordained to be the family's fourth generation doctor. His father had enrolled Reggie, at his birth, in the Harvard Medical school where Reggie's father, grandfather and great grandfather had matriculated. Such was the certainty of Reggie's heritage, his occupational destiny.

The hitch, of course, was that young Reggie had no intention of becoming a doctor. His life aim throughout our high school years was NOT to follow those footsteps. His strategy was simple: FAIL high school. My good friend was incredibly successful at not being successful. I remember him as a happy, adventurous classmate with a mighty mission. Opposite from the rest of us, the more dismal his report card the more joyous he would be. Still, he was so bright he had difficulty failing. Teachers knew that his mind was not a failing mind. They bent more to their concept of his natural intelligence than to his test results or his haphazard homework submissions. Indeed, we graduated together in spite of his failing efforts. Yet he triumphed...doing poorly enough to resoundly erase his premature Harvard enrollment.

Soon after our graduation I went off to college in Ohio and lost all contact with Reggie until only a few years ago. That's when our high school got the idea, no doubt to raise money, to sponsor some class reunions. I was invited to the forty year gathering.

Somehow Reggie found my whereabouts, still in Ohio, and telephoned me. He urged me to come to New York for the reunion, stay at his place on Manhatten's upper west side. I turned down the offer but I couldn't resist the question, "Reggie, are you a doctor?" The phone went silent for a few beats before he answered.

"I'm in medical research. No standard patient practice...basically a cancer fighter."

"Where the hell did you go to medical school?" I asked.

"It's a long story" he said.

"Where!" I persisted.

"I went to an academy in France...outside of Paris. They exist for people like me, poor students with wealthy, committed fathers."

"It sounds like your father trumped you," I said.

"I guess you could say that. But things change," he said, "I grew to like the idea of research science, especially in the health field. I'm doing some cutting edge stuff. I love my work; frustrating...but exciting. My father died only a year ago. We became friends. He changed too, became quite proud of me, as if medical research was the epitome of the profession. I have two sons. One became a race car driver and the other his chief mechanic. They do business things now. Dad was close to the boys...called them 'Auto Medics.' He sold the old brownstone about ten years ago, but continued to rent the top floor until the day he died."

Reggie asked about me and I gave a brief accounting of my life highlights. Our whole conversation lasted about as long as it takes to read this accounting of it.

This brief sketch, not more than a few snapshots in Reggie's six decades, tells an apropos story of how we can amend our absurdities to form and frame a positive view of a life journey. As a youngster, Reggie's absurdities centered around school failure, to succeed his aim of not being a doctor. But the absurdities failed. He fell short of that objective. He is a doctor. Along the way he altered his failure-centered absurdities to ones that accept doctoring...but in a non-traditional sense. That is the magic of the *significance* we give to the events in our lives. We are their spin doctor, pardon the pun. We can alter the significance of what happens to us, our absurdities, to affirm our path whether that path is by choice, by accident or by predetermination.

There are many events in our lives that we cannot control, or cannot control entirely. Some of these events seem disadvantageous on their surface. A flood destroys our home. A loved one dies. A virus infects us. A partner turns mean or succumbs to alcohol or to someone else. A college rejects us. A friend betrays us. A competitor beats us. A job is lost. On and on, we are fated to ride a streetcar no one desires. Yet the significance we give to every one of these events is entirely our doing. Others may urge a significance for us. A creed or religion or nation or mother or daughter or philosophy or TV commercial may urge a significance upon us...that we may well accept. We may delegate the significance-making to another, or to many others. But in the end we are the *only* ones who give or accept a significance to the events in our lives. We alone can alter that significance at our will. Is this absurd? Of course it is. But this is the absurdity of absurdity therapy. Universal? Of course not. Surely there are some who reject this therapy on its face, on its absurd absurdities! Naturally, it is our belief and experience that absurdity therapy can bridge many people over the troubled waters in their lives.

FINALE: A PRIMER IN NINE SHORT PARAGRAPHS

There is no significance or meaning given to anything in our existence that is universally accepted by everyone: No Universal Meanings. This is important because if there were universal meanings, they would - most likely - NOT be changeable. Thus the meaning we give to anything that happens in our lives can be changed by us at any time or any place of our choosing. We are the master of what we believe. This is why we call our beliefs ABSURDITIES...which simply means they are not universally accepted.

The way we feel is generated by our absurdities. Our feelings come from what we believe (absurdity) about what happens in our lives. These events in our lives do NOT create our feelings...but what we believe about these events is where our feelings are born. Absurdities generate feelings.

Some of our absurdities come from the influence of other people. Some may come from the influence of our other absurdities. Most absurdities are generated by ourselves, we are their makers. Whatever the source of an absurdity, however, once we take it on as our own, it is ours...we own it...and we can discard it or change it in any way or at any time we choose.

The way we behave is most often generated by our feelings. Joy will motivate a different set of behaviors than anger...or depression...or anxiety. Since our feelings emanate from our absurdities, it is fair to say that our absurdities give rise to our feelings and the way those feelings have us behave.

Feelings fall on a range from Deep Denial to Firm Affirmation of our life goals. Negative or denial feelings lead us away from where we want to go in life. Feelings of affirmation lead us toward where we want to go in life.

Some of our absurdities, especially denial absurdities can be difficult to recall. They may even be hidden by guardian absurdities. However, there are a number of techniques for calling up these illusive absurdities. The more common negative or denial feelings or behaviors are depression, anxiety, anger, loss, jealousy, addiction, stress, compulsions. There are absurdities commonly associated with each of these denial feelings that can make them easier to recall and deal with.

Our ability to alter our absurdities is a way of defining a flexible mind, as opposed to a mind that is stuck with a set of absurdities it cannot change, and that may be generating some hurtful feelings and behaviors.

We have the power to alter any of our absurdities. In fact, altering some of our absurdities is a daily occurrence. Therefore, if an absurdity is hurting us...keeping us from where we want to go...we have the ability or power to recall it and to change it into an absurdity that affirms us...helps us get to where we want to go. Most of us can alter our negative absurdities on our own - without professional assistance.

This is the process by which absurdity therapy can help freshen up our lives, help us stay on the path of our desire.

FORM 1

━━◦◦◦◦━━

CHANGING AN ABSURDITY
THE OPPOSITE TECHNIQUE

Write down the absurdity that seems to be causing the problem. Then, at the bottom of the form, write down the OPPOSITE of that absurdity. Then in the INTERIM spaces, write down two absurdities that are between the problem absurdity and its opposite.

THE TROUBLING ABSURDITY:

_____

_____

_____

AN INTERIM ABSURDITY:

_____

_____

_____

AN INTERIM ABSURDITY (closer to the opposite):

_____

_____

_____

THE OPPOSITE ABSURDITY:

_____

_____

_____

SAMPLE FORM 1

CHANGING AN ABSURDITY
THE OPPOSITE TECHNIQUE:

Write down the absurdity that seems to be causing the problem. Then, at the bottom of the form, write down the OPPOSITE of that absurdity. Then in the IN-TERIM spaces, write down two absurdities that are between the problem absurdity and its opposite.

THE TROUBLING ABSURDITY:
My boyfriend must never be seen with another girl.

AN INTERIM ABSURDITY:
If my boyfriend wants to go out with another girl, he better discuss it with me way ahead of time and get my permission.

AN INTERIM ABSURDITY (Closer to the opposite):
If my boyfriend goes out with another girl, he should tell me about it ahead of time.

THE OPPOSITE ABSURDITY:
My boyfriend can be seen with another girl any time and it's okay with me.

REFERENCES

Adler, A. *Understanding Human Nature*. New York: Greenberg, 1927.

Bandura, A. *Social Learning Theory*. New York: Prentice-Hall, 1976.

Bard, J. A. *Rational-Emotive Therapy in Practice*. Champaign, IL:Research Press, 1980.

Beck, A. T. *Cognitive Therapy and the Emotional Disorders*. New York: International Universities Press, 1972.

Bernard, M.E., and Joyce, M.R. *Rational-Emotive Therapy with Children and Adolescents*. New York: Wiley-Interscience, 1984.

Burns, D. *Feeling Good: The New Mood Therapy*. New York: Wm. Morrow & Co., 1980.

Burns, D. *The Feeling Good Handbook*. New York: Wm. Morrow & Co., 1989.

Ellis. A. *Reason and Emotion in Psychotherapy*. New York: Lyle Stuart, 1962.

Ellis, A. *Humanistic Psychotherapy: The Rational-Emotive Approach*. New York: Julian Press, and McGraw-Hill Paperbacks, 1973.

Ellis, A, and Becker, I. *A Guide to Personal Happiness*. Hollywood: Wilshire Book Co., 1982.

Ellis, A., and Dryden, W. *The Practice of Rational-Emotive Therapy*. New York: Springer Publishing Co., 1987.

Ellis, A., and Grieger, R. *Handbook of Rational-Emotive Therapy*. (Vol. 1) New York: Springer Publishing Co., 1977.

Ellis, A. and Grieger, R. *Handbook of Rational-Emotive Therapy*. (Vol. 2) New York: Springer Publishing Co., 1986,

Ellis, A., and Harper, R.A. *A New Guide to Rational Living*. 3rd rev. ed. North Hollywood, CA: Wilshire Book Co.., 1997.

Frankl, V. *Man's Search for Meaning*. New York: Washington Square Press, 1966.

Grieger, R.M., and Boyd, J. *Rational-Emotive Therapy: A Skills-Based Approach*. New York: Van Nostrand Reinhold, 1980.

Haley, J. *Strategies of Psychotherapy*. New York: Grune and Stratton, 1963.

Haley, J. *Problem Solving Therapy*. San Francisco: Jossey-Bass, 1976.

Hauck, P. *Brief Counseling with RET*. Philadelphia: Westminister, 1980.

Hauck, P. *Overcoming Frustration and Anger*. Philadelphia: Westminister Press, 1974.

Lazarus, A.A. *Behavior Therapy and Beyond*. New York: McGraw-Hill, 1971.

Lazarus, A.A. (Ed.), *Multimodal Behavior Therapy*. New York: Springer Publishing Co., 1976.

Mahoney, M.J. *Cognition and Behavior Modification*. Cambridge, MA: Ballinger, 1974.

Walen, S.R., DiGiuseppe, R., and Dryden, W. *A Practitioner's Guide to Rational-Emotive Therapy*. New York: Oxford University Press, 1992.

Wessler, R.A., and Wessler, R.L. *The Principles and Practice of Rational-Emotive Therapy*. San Francisco: Jossey-Bass, 1980

NOTES

NOTES

NOTES

NOTES